the FREEDOM SHRINE® documents

The Freedom Shrine and The Exchange Clubs

The Freedom Shrine is a collection of 28 original historic American documents photographically reproduced and displayed throughout America to remind its citizens that the freedom they enjoy today is the product of the determination and sacrifice of courageous men of yesterday. The Shrine is an exclusive project of the Exchange Clubs — groups of business and professional men in communities across America who are banded together to provide helpful service to their fellow citizens. The Clubs are non-profit, non-sectarian, and non-political. Unlike other service organizations, the Exchange Clubs confine their activity to within the United States, Puerto Rico, and the U.S. Virgin Islands. The Freedom Shrine is only one of several programs sponsored by Exchange to promote good citizenship and encourage a greater appreciation of their American heritage among our nation's young people. Exchange Club members, whose motto is "Unity for Service," also sponsor a great number of other programs to aid and assist their fellowman. The Exchange Clubs maintain a National Headquarters in Toledo, Ohio.

How to Use This Book

This book was designed to be read and used in conjunction with the Freedom Shrine. Thus, a small photograph of the historical document as it appears on the Freedom Shrine is included with each of the printed texts on the following pages. In this way, the photo can be used as an aid in finding the document on the Shrine or vice versa. The numbers appearing with the photos and used on the Contents page also help locate the original documents as they appear on the Shrine. However, the numbering system is optional and may not be found on every Freedom Shrine.

Foreword

This is a great book . . . great because it was shaped and written by men whose courage, determination, wisdom, and action — like indomitable seeds — took root in the minds of men and flowered into ideas that have transcended the generations. Some of the 28 documents which are printed on the following pages contain, even to this day, some of the most moving and readable passages ever written. Others are archaic in language, imperfect in style, even burdensome in terms of pure weight of words. But that is not why they have survived the fluctuating tides of time.

They have survived and are rightfully preserved because they indelibly mark what were irreversible beginnings and often turbulent turning points of enduring consequence. They also reveal the character of men who, in the face of staggering odds, succeeded in doing what few men have done — transformed a dream into reality — created a bastion of freedom and then protected and perfected it. That is the significance of these documents.

That is why The National Exchange Club in 1949 decided to display these documents in an appropriate way so that the beneficiaries of these historic realities could see them in their original form . . . as they were first written . . . and experience that sense of awe which all men feel in the presence of the past. They were selected carefully and their authenticity established beyond all reasonable doubt. Precise photographic reproductions were made from the original documents preserved in the National Archives and the Library of Congress. Thus the Freedom Shrine was born.

And thus has America — especially its younger citizens — been given the opportunity to study the actualities of our Nation's history. Literally thousands of Freedom Shrines have been installed in schools and public buildings in every corner of our land by the hundreds of Exchange Clubs throughout the United States, Puerto Rico, and the U.S. Virgin Islands. Perpetuated in this way, the program has become one of the most successful ever undertaken by any service organization.

Because of this and because even the most enduring of man's creations become obscured by the erosion of time and circumstance, this book was published to enable those who view the Freedom Shrine to more clearly see and understand the words before them. Many of the documents, because they are original and authentic, are partially obliterated or virtually illegible . . . some because of early mishandling and atmospheric deterioration . . . others because the penmanship of our forefathers, like many of us today, is almost undecipherable. Quaint spellings and, compared to current practice, the odd use of capitalization as well as archaic shapes of 18th Century script also make direct reading of the original documents somewhat difficult.

Although the authenticity of the documents, even to the point of authentic but incorrect spellings, is faithfully preserved in the printed versions contained in this book, it is hoped that their transformation into a more modern and readable type face will make them even more meaningful. The texts are the result of the most careful research . . . research that incidentally uncovered numerous errors, omissions and erroneous additions in what were previously considered to be authentic printed versions of the documents.

It should also be noted that although all of the documents, based on the best available research, are printed in this book in their entirety, only portions of seven are displayed on the Freedom Shrine. That is because only these portions of the original documents remain to this day. The documents are Patrick Henry's Instructions to George Rogers Clark, the Treaty of Paris, Washington's First Inaugural Address, Washington's Farewell Address (First Draft), Jefferson's First Inaugural Address, the Monroe Doctrine, and The Emancipation Proclamation.

In a sense then, this publication can be considered a guidebook . . . a guidebook to the past, as well as to the present and to the future. For the documents of the Freedom Shrine, although culled from the past, represent foundation stones which permit the present, as we know it, to exist and the future, as we dream it, to be attainable.

UNITY FOR SERVICE · NATIONAL EXCHANGE CLUB

FREEDOM SHRINE

PRESENTED BY
THE EXCHANGE CLUBS

Contents

The documents, as they are presented in this book, are in chronological order.

Library of Congress Catalog Card Number 73-84292

Acknowledgements

Preparation of Freedom Shrine Documents
—National Archives, Library of Congress,
Princeton University Library,
and Massachusetts State Library

Book Design and Production
—William and Howard Associates

Illustrations
—Timothy J. Cross and Donald E. Raden

Typography (Optima)
—Harlan Typographic

Lithography
—Len Beach Associates, Inc.

Printed in U.S.A.

MAYFLOWER COMPACT
Governor Bradford's Account

The Mayflower Compact, first written Constitution in America, was signed by 41 adult, male passengers aboard the Mayflower, November 11, 1620, off Cape Cod, prior to the landing at Plymouth. This version by William Bradford, second Governor of the Colony, is taken from page 54 of his "History of the Plymouth Plantation" written during the years 1630-1648. The whereabouts of the original Compact is unknown. It is thought to have been destroyed by fire during the colony's early years.

1

. . . Acte by them done (this their condition considered) might be as firme as any patent; and in some respects more sure.

The forme was as followeth,

In ye name of God Amen. We whose names are underwriten, the Loyall subjects of our dread Soveraigne Lord King James, by ye grace of God, of great Britaine, Franc, & Ireland King, defender of ye faith, &c

Haveing undertaken, for ye glorie of God, and advancemente of ye christian faith and honour of our king & countrie, a voyage to plant ye first colonie in ye Northerne parts of Virginia. Doe by these presents solemnly & mutualy in ye presence of God, and one of another, covenant, & combine our selves togeather into a civill body politick; for our better ordering, & preservation & furtherance of ye ends aforesaid; and by Vertue hereof to Enacte, Constitute, and frame Shuch just & equall lawes, ordinances, Acts, constitutions, & offices, from time to time, as shall be thought most meete & convenient for ye generall good of ye colonie: Unto which we promise all due submission and obedience. In witness whereof we have hereunder subscribed our names at Cap-Codd ye.11. of November, in ye year of ye raigne of our soveraigne Lord king James of England, France, & Ireland ye eighteenth, and of Scotland ye fiftie-fourth.

Ano: Dom. 1620

After this they chose, or rather confirmed Mr. John Carver (a man Godly & well approved amongst them) their Governour for that year. And after they had provided a place for their goods, or comone store, (which were long in unlading for want of boats, foulnes of ye winter weather, and sicknes of diverce) and begune some small cottages for their habitation; as time would admitte they mette and consulted of lawes; & orders, both for their civill, & military Governmente, as ye necessitie of their condition did require, still adding thereunto as urgent occasion in severall times, and as cases did require.

In these hard & difficulte beginnings they found some discontents & murmurings arise amongst some, and mutinous speeches & carriags in other; but they were soon quelled, & overcome, by ye wisdome, patience, and just & equall carrage of things, by ye Govr: and better part wch clave faithfully togeather in ye maine: But that which was most sadd, & lamentable, was, that in .2. or .3. moneths time halfe of their company dyed, especialy in Jan: & February, being ye depth of winter, and wanting houses & other comforts; being infected with ye scurvie & . . .

THE DECLARATION OF INDEPENDENCE
Jefferson's "Rough Draft"

Thomas Jefferson, author of the Declaration of Independence, wrote the "Rough Draft" reproduced here. Changes suggested by Benjamin Franklin and John Adams, indicated in the margins of the original as being in their handwriting, are shown here in regular parenthesis and footnoted. For purposes of readability, unidentified changes by other members of the committee of five named to draft it have been incorporated into the printed text without notation. Passages in square parenthesis are exactly as they appear on the original. The original is in the Library of Congress at Washington.

2

A Declaration
by the Representatives of the UNITED STATES
OF AMERICA, in General Congress assembled.

When in the course of human events it becomes necessary for one people to dissolve the political bands which have connected them with another, and to assume among the powers of the earth the separate and equal station to which the laws of nature & of nature's god entitle them, a decent respect to the opinions of mankind requires that they should declare the causes which impel them to the separation.

We hold these truths to be self-evident: that all men are created equal, that they are endowed by their creator with certain [inherent &] inalienable rights; that among these are life, liberty, & the pursuit of happiness; that to secure these rights, governments are instituted among men, deriving their just powers from the consent of the governed; that whenever any form of government becomes destructive of these ends, it is the right of the people to alter or to abolish it, & to institute new government, laying it's foundation on such principles & organising it's powers in such form, as to them shall seem most likely to effect their safety & happiness. prudence indeed will dictate that governments long established should not be changed for light & transient causes: and accordingly all experience hath shewn that mankind are more disposed to suffer while evils are sufferable, than to right themselves by abolishing the forms to which they are accustomed. but when a long train of abuses & usurpations, [begun at a distinguished period, &] pursuing invariably the same object, evinces a design to reduce them (†under absolute Despotism), it is their right, it is their duty, to throw off such government & to provide new guards for their future security. such has been the patient sufferance of these colonies; & such is now the necessity which constrains them to alter [expunge] their former systems of government. the history of the present (‡King of Great Britain) is a history of repeated [unremitting] injuries and usurpations,

(among which appears no solitary fact to contradict the uniform tenor of the rest, but all having [have] in direct object the establishment of an absolute tyranny over these states. to prove this, let facts be submitted to a candid world, [for the truth of which we pledge a faith yet unsullied by falsehood.]

he has refused his assent to laws the most wholesome and necessary for the public good:

he has forbidden his governors to pass laws of immediate & pressing importance, unless suspended in their operation till his assent should be obtained: and when so suspended, he has utterly neglected to attend to them.

he has refused to pass other laws for the accomodation of large districts of people unless those people would relinquish the right of representation in the legislature, a right inestimable to them, & formidable to tyrants only:

he has dissolved Representative houses repeatedly, for opposing with manly firmness his invasions on the rights of the people:

he has refused for a long (‡time after such Dissolutions) to cause others to be elected, whereby the Legislative powers, incapable of annihilation, have returned to the people at large for their exercise, the state remaining in the mean time exposed to all the dangers of invasion from without, &, convulsions within:

he has endeavored to prevent the population of these states; for that purpose obstructing the laws for naturalisation of foreigners; refusing to pass others to encourage their migration hither; & raising the conditions of new appropriations of lands:

he has [suffered] the administration of justice [totally to cease in some of these states] refusing his assent to laws for establishing judiciary powers:

he has made [our] judges dependant on his will

11

alone, for the tenure of their offices, and the amount (†& payment) of their salaries:

he has erected a multitude of new offices [by a self-assumed power,] & sent hither swarms of officers to harrass our people & eat out their substance:

he has kept among us in times of peace standing armies [& ships of war without the consent of our Legislature:]

he has affected to render the military, independent of & superior to the civil power:

he has combined with others to subject us to a jurisdiction foreign to our Constitution and unacknoleged by our laws; giving his assent to their acts of pretended legislation, for quartering large bodies of armed troops among us:

for protecting them by a mock-trial from punishments for any murders which they should commit on the inhabitants of these states:

for cutting off our trade with all parts of the world;

for imposing taxes on us without our consent;

for depriving us in many cases of the benefits of trial by jury;

for transporting us beyond seas to be tried for pretended offenses;

for abolishing the free system of English laws in a neighboring province, establishing therein an arbitrary government and enlarging its boundaries so as to render it at once an example & fit instrument for introducing the same absolute rule to these colonies: ists:

†Dr. Franklin's handwriting
‡Mr. Adam's handwriting

THE DECLARATION OF INDEPENDENCE

The draft of the Declaration of Independence was reported to the Continental Congress on June 28, 1776. On July 2 debate on it began and two days later, July 4, it was adopted. It was not until July 19 that Congress ordered the Declaration to be engrossed on parchment. It was signed by the Members of Congress present on August 2 and later by a few others. The original document is in the National Archives at Washington.

3

In CONGRESS, July 4, 1776. The unanimous Declaration of the thirteen united States of America,

When in the Course of human events, it becomes necessary for one people to dissolve the political bands which have connected them with another, and to assume among the powers of the earth, the separate and equal station to which the Laws of Nature and of Nature's God entitle them, a decent respect to the opinions of mankind requires that they should declare the causes which impel them to the separation. ——————— We hold these truths to be self-evident, that all men are created equal, that they are endowed by their Creator with certain unalienable Rights, that among these are Life, Liberty and the pursuit of Happiness. ——————— That to secure these rights, Governments are instituted among Men, deriving their just powers from the consent of the governed, ——————— That whenever any Form of Government becomes destructive of these ends, it is the Right of the People to alter or to abolish it, and to institute new Government, laying its foundation on such principles and organizing its powers in such form, as to them shall seem most likely to effect their Safety and Happiness. Prudence, indeed, will dictate that Governments long established should not be changed for light and transient causes; and accordingly all experience hath shewn, that mankind are more disposed to suffer, while evils are sufferable, than to right themselves by abolishing the forms to which they are accustomed. But when along train of abuses and usurpations, pursuing invariably the same Object evinces a design to reduce them under absolute Despotism, it is their right, it is their duty, to throw off such Government, and to provide new Guards for their future security. ——————— Such has been the patient sufferance of these Colonies; and such is now the necessity which constrains them to alter their former Systems of Government. The history of the present King of Great Britain is a history of repeated injuries and usurpations, all having in direct object the establishment of an absolute Tyranny over these States. To prove this, let Facts be submitted to a candid world. ——————— —————— He has refused his Assent to Laws, the most wholesome and necessary for the public good. ——————— He has forbidden his Governors to pass Laws of immediate and pressing importance, unless suspended in their operation till his Assent should be obtained; and when so suspended, he has utterly neglected to attend to them. ——————— —————— He has refused to pass other Laws for the accommodation of large districts of people, unless those people would relinquish the right of Representation in the Legislature, a right inestimable to them and formidable to tyrants only. ——————— He has called together legislative bodies at places unusual, uncomfortable, and distant from the depository of their public Records, for the sole purpose of fatiguing them into compliance with his measures. ——————— He has dissolved Representative Houses repeatedly, for opposing with manly firmness his invasions on the rights of the people. ——————— He has refused for along time, after such dissolutions, to cause others to be elected; whereby the Legislative powers, incapable of Annihilation, have returned to the People at large for their exercise; the State remaining in the mean time exposed to all the dangers of invasion from without, and convulsions within. ——————— He has endeavoured to prevent the population of these States; for that purpose obstructing the Laws for Naturalization of Foreigners; refusing to pass others to encourage their migrations hither, and raising the conditions of new Appropriations of Lands. ——————— He has obstructed the Administration of Justice, by refusing his Assent to Laws for establishing Judiciary powers. ——————— He has made Judges dependent on his Will alone, for the tenure of their offices, and the amount and payment of their salaries. ——————— He has erected a multitude of New Offices, and sent hither swarms of Officers to harrass our people, and eat out their substance. ——————— He has kept among us, in times of peace, Standing Armies without the Consent of our legislatures. ——————— He has affected to render the Military independent of and superior to the Civil power. ——————— He has combined with others to subject us to a jurisdiction foreign to our constitution, and unacknowledged by our laws; giving his Assent to their Acts of pretended Legislation: ——————— For Quartering large bodies of armed troops among us: ——————— For protecting them by amock Trial, from punishment for any Murders which they should commit on the Inhabitants of these States: ———————

For cutting off our Trade with all parts of the world: —————— For imposing Taxes on us without our Consent: —————— For depriving us in many cases, of the benefits of Trial by Jury: —————— For transporting us beyond Seas to be tried for pretended offences: —————— For abolishing the free System of English Laws in a neighbouring Province, establishing therein an Arbitrary government, and enlarging its Boundaries so as to render it at once an example and fit instrument for introducing the same absolute rule into these Colonies: —————— For taking away our Charters, abolishing our most valuable Laws, and altering fundamentally the Forms of our Governments: —————— For suspending our own Legislatures, and declaring themselves invested with power to legislate for us in all cases whatsoever. —————— He has abdicated Government here, by declaring us out of his Protection and waging War against us. —————— He has plundered our seas, ravaged our Coasts, burnt our towns, and destroyed the Lives of our people. —————— He is at this time transporting large Armies of foreign Mercenaries to compleat the works of death, desolation and tyranny, already begun with circumstances of Cruelty & perfidy scarcely paralleled in the most barbarous ages, and totally unworthy the Head of a civilized nation. —————— He has constrained our fellow Citizens taken Captive on the high Seas to bear Arms against their Country, to become the executioners of their friends and Brethern, or to fall themselves by their Hands. —————— He has excited domestic insurrections amongst us, and has endeavoured to bring on the inhabitants of our frontiers, the merciless Indian Savages, whose known rule of warfare, is an undistinguished destruction of all ages, sexes and conditions. In every stage of these Oppressions We —————— have Petitioned for Redress in the most humble terms: Our repeated Petitions have been answered only by repeated injury. A Prince, whose character is thus marked by every act which may define a Tyrant, is unfit to be the ruler of a free people. Nor have We been wanting in attentions to our Brittish brethern. We have warned them from time to time of attempts by their legislature to extend an unwarrantable jurisdiction over us. We have reminded them of the circumstances of our emigration and settlement here. We have appealed to their native justice and magnanimity, and we have conjured them by the ties of our common kindred to disavow these usurpations, which, would inevitably interrupt our connections and correspondence They too have been deaf to the voice of justice and of consanguinity. We must, therefore, acquiesce in the necessity, which denounces our Separation, and hold them, as we hold the rest of mankind, Enemies in War, in Peace Friends. ——————

We, therefore, the Representatives of the united States of America, in General Congress, Assembled, appealing to the Supreme Judge of the world for the rectitude of our intentions, do, in the Name, and by Authority of the good People of these Colonies, solemnly publish and declare, That these United Colonies are, and of Right ought to be Free and Independent States; that they are Absolved from all Allegiance to the British Crown, and that all political connection between them and the State of Great Britain, is and ought to be totally dissolved; and that as Free and Independent States, they have full power to levy War, conclude Peace, contract Alliances, establish Commerce, and to do all other Acts and Things which Independent States may of right do. ——————

And for the support of this Declaration, with a firm reliance on the protection of divine Providence, we mutually pledge to each other our Lives, our Fortunes and our sacred Honor.

THE SIGNERS OF THE
DECLARATION OF INDEPENDENCE

Name	Born—Died	Colony	Profession
John Adams	1735-1826	Mass.	Lawyer
Samuel Adams	1722-1803	Mass.	Businessman
Josiah Bartlett	1729-1795	N. H.	Physician
Carter Braxton	1736-1797	Va.	Planter
Charles Carroll	1737-1832	Md.	Lawyer
Samuel Chase	1741-1811	Md.	Lawyer
Abraham Clark	1726-1794	N. J.	Politician
George Clymer	1739-1813	Pa.	Banker
William Ellery	1727-1820	R. I.	Lawyer
William Floyd	1734-1821	N. Y.	Farmer
Benjamin Franklin	1706-1790	Pa.	Publisher
Elbridge Gerry	1744-1814	Mass.	Merchant
Button Gwinnett	1735(?)-1777	Ga.	Merchant
Lyman Hall	1724-1790	Ga.	Physician
John Hancock	1737-1793	Mass.	Merchant
Benjamin Harrison	1726-1791	Va.	Planter
John Hart	1711(?)-1779	N. J.	Farmer
Joseph Hewes	1730-1779	N. C.	Merchant
Thomas Heyward, Jr.	1746-1809	S. C.	Lawyer
William Hooper	1742-1790	N. C.	Lawyer
Stephen Hopkins	1707-1785	R. I.	Merchant
Francis Hopkinson	1737-1791	N. J.	Lawyer
Samuel Huntington	1731-1796	Conn.	Lawyer
Thomas Jefferson	1743-1826	Va.	Planter
Francis Lightfoot Lee	1734-1797	Va.	Planter
Richard Henry Lee	1732-1794	Va.	Planter
Francis Lewis	1713-1802	N. Y.	Merchant
Philip Livingston	1716-1778	N. Y.	Merchant
Thomas Lynch, Jr.	1749-1779	S. C.	Planter
Thomas McKean	1734-1817	Dela.	Lawyer
Arthur Middleton	1742-1787	S. C.	Lawyer
Lewis Morris	1726-1798	N. Y.	Landowner
Robert Morris	1734-1806	Pa.	Financier
John Morton	1724-1777	Pa.	Farmer
Thomas Nelson	1738-1789	Va.	Planter
William Paca	1740-1799	Md.	Lawyer
Robert Treat Paine	1731-1814	Mass.	Lawyer
John Penn	1740-1788	N. C.	Lawyer
George Read	1733-1798	Dela.	Lawyer
Caesar Rodney	1728-1784	Dela.	Planter
George Ross	1730-1779	Pa.	Lawyer
Benjamin Rush	1745-1813	Pa.	Physician
Edward Rutledge	1749-1800	S. C.	Planter
Roger Sherman	1721-1793	Conn.	Merchant
James Smith	1719(?)-1806	Pa.	Lawyer
Richard Stockton	1730-1781	N. J.	Lawyer
Thomas Stone	1743-1787	Md.	Lawyer
George Taylor	1716-1781	Pa.	Iron-maker
Matthew Thornton	1714(?)-1803	N. H.	Physician
George Walton	1741-1804	Ga.	Lawyer
William Whipple	1730-1785	N. H.	Merchant
William Williams	1731-1811	Conn.	Merchant
James Wilson	1742-1798	Pa.	Lawyer
John Witherspoon	1723-1794	N. J.	Clergyman
Oliver Wolcott	1726-1797	Conn.	Politician-Soldier
George Wythe	1726-1806	Va.	Lawyer

BENJAMIN FRANKLIN'S EPITAPH

Franklin wrote out a copy of his epitaph — one of the most famous in the English language — and presented it to Samuel Morris in Philadelphia on August 31, 1776. The original manuscript belongs to Colonel Richard Gimbel.

4

The Body of
B. Franklin, Printer,
Like the Cover of an old Book,
Its Contents torn out,
And stript of its Lettering & Gilding,
Lies here, Food for Worms.-
But the Work shall not be lost;
For it will, as he believ'd, appear once more
In a new and more elegant Edition
Corrected and improved
By the Author. —

1

Given by B Franklin to Sam. Morris
August 31 1776 —————

It is his own hand writing

PATRICK HENRY'S INSTRUCTIONS TO GEORGE ROGERS CLARK

In December 1778, Patrick Henry, Governor of Virginia, sent instructions to George Rogers Clark, commander of American forces in the Illinois country, stressing the importance of the friendship of the French and Indians to the American cause in the Revolution. The original document is in the National Archives at Washington.

5

Sir,   Decr. 12, 1778

You are to retain the Command of the troops now at the several posts in the county of Illinois and on the Wabash, which fall within the limits of the County now erected and called Illinois County, which troops marched out with, and have been embodied by you. You are also to take the Command of five other Companies, raised under the act of Assembly which I send herewith, and which if completed, as I hope they will be speedily, will have orders to join you without loss of time, and are likewise to be under your command; With your whole force you are to protect the Inhabitants of the County, & as occasions may serve, annoy the enemy.

It is thought that the Indian Nations may be overawed and inclined to peace with us, by the Adoption of proper measures with you. Or if that cannot be effected, that such of them as send out parties towards our Frontiers on this side of the Ohio, may be chastised by detachments from your quarter. For this purpose it will behove you to watch their motions, and to consider, that one great advantage expected from your situation is to prevent the Indians from warring on this side of Ohio.

In order more effectually to prevent this, you are to establish such posts in different parts of the Country as you judge best for your troops to occupy.

I consider your further success as depending upon the goodwill and friendship of the Frenchmen and Indians who inhabit your part of the Commonwealth. With their concurrence great things may be accomplished. But their animosity will spoil the fair prospect which your past successes have opened. You will therefore spare no pains to conciliate the affections of the French and Indians. Let them see and feel the advantages of being fellow citizens and freemen.

Guard most carefully against every infringement of their property, particularly with respect to land, as our enemies have alarmed them as to that. Strict, and even severe, discipline with your soldiers may be essential, to preserve from injury those whom they were sent to protect and conciliate. This is a great and capital matter, and I confide that you will never lose sight of it, or suffer your troops to injure any person without feeling the punishment due to the offense. The honor and interest of the state are deeply concerned in this & the attachment of the French & Indians depends upon a due observance of it.

John Todd Esq.ʳ being appointed County Lieutenant according to Law during pleasure, with ample powers chiefly confined to the civil Department, will have Directions to act in Concert with you wherever it can be done. On your part, you will omit no opportunity to give him the necessary Cooperation of the Troops where the case necessarily requires it. Much will depend upon the mutual assistances you may occasionally afford each other in your respective Departments. And I trust that a sincere Cordiality will subsist between you. The contrary will prove highly detrimental.

Some measures will be fallen on for carrying on a Trade to supply Inhabitants of your County. You will afford the Agents such aid or protection from time to time as affairs require & your Circumstances will permit.

I send you herewith some Copies of the Act of Government & Bill of Rights, together with the french Alliance. These will serve to shew our new friends; the Ground upon which they are to stand, & the Support to be expected from their Countrymen of France. Equal Liberty & Happiness are the objects, to a participation of which we invite them. upon a fair presumption that the people about Detroit have similar Inclinations with those at Illinois & Wabash I think it probable, that they may be brought to expell their British Masters. & become fellow Citizens of a free State. I recommend this to your Serious Consideration, & to consult with some confidential persons on the Subject. Perhaps Mr. Gibault, the Priest (to whom this country owes many Thanks for his Zeal & Services) may promote this affair. But I refer it to you to select the proper persons to advise with & to act as occasion offers. But you are to push at any favourable Occurance which Fortune may present to you. For our peace & Safety are not secure while the Enemy are so near as Detroit.

I wish you to testify to all the subjects of Spain upon every occasion, the high regard, & sincere friendship of this Commonwealth towards them. And I hope it will soon be manifest that mutual advantages will derive from the neighbourhood of the Virginians & the Subjects of his, Catholic Majesty.

I must observe to you, that your Situation is critical. Far detached from the Body of your Country, placed among French Spaniards & Indian nations Strangers to our people, anxiously watching your Actions & Behaviour, & ready to receive Impressions favorable, or not so, of our Commonwealth &—its Government, which Impression will be hard to remove & will produce lasting Good or ill Effects to your Country; These Considerations will make you cautious & Circumspect. I feel the Delicacy & difficulty of your Situation, but I doubt not your Virtue will accomplish the Arduous Work with Honor to yourself & advantage to the Commonwealth. The Advice & assistance of discreet good men will be highly necessary. For at the Distance of your County, I cannot be consulted. General Discretionary powers therefore are given you to act for the best in all Cases where these Instructions are Silent, & the Law has made no provision.

I desire your particular attention to Mrs. Rocheblare & her Children, & that you suffer them to want for nothing. let Mr. Rocheblare's property which was taken be restored to his Lady so far as it can be done. — You, have the Sum of sixty pounds — sent for her use in case you can't find her husband's Effects to restore.

Prudence requires that provisions be laid in to subsist the Troops you have & those to be expected to arrive with you Colonel Bowman has contracted to deliver 35,000lb Bear Bacon at Kentucky, But Bread must be had at Illinois. You will provide it if possible before the arrival of the Troops, or the necessity to buy it becomes gener-

ally known as perhaps advantages may be taken by raising the price. Lay up also a good Stock of powder & Lead.

There is a Cargo of Goods at a Spanish post near you belonging either to the Continent or this State. Rather than let your Troops be naked, you are to take a Supply for them out of these goods. But this is not to be done but in Case of absolute necessity. Let an exact Account be Kept of what is used & let me receive it.

In your Negotiations or Treaties with the Indians, you will be assisted by Mr. Todd. Let the treatys be confined to the Subject of amity & peace with our people, & not to touch the Subject of Lands. You may accept of any Services they offer, for expelling the English from Detroit & elsewhere. In case you find presents to the Savages neces-

sary, make them sparingly as possible, letting them know our stock of Goods is small at present, but by means of our Trade with the french & other nations we expect plenty of Goods before it is long.

Lieutenant Colonel Montgomery will convey to you ten thousand pounds for payment of the Troops & for other Matters requiring money; In the Distribution of money you will be carefull to keep exact accounts from time to time & take Security where it is proper.

I am, Sir
yr.hble. Serv
P. Henry

WASHINGTON'S LETTER TO COL. NICOLA

Soon after Washington's arrival at Newburgh, N.Y. in 1782, he received a memorandum from Colonel Lewis Nicola, one of his oldest and most dignified Commanders. It contained the explosive suggestion of a coup d'etat to make Washington king. Dissatisfaction within the Army stemmed directly from Congress' failure to provide it with food, clothing or pay after its recent victories against the British. The suggestion called for a betrayal of the very principles for which the war had been fought. Washington's famous reply repudiating Nicola's idea ended completely any talk of an American monarchy. The original letter is in the Library of Congress.

6

Newburgh May 22, '82

Sir:

   With a mixture of great surprise & astonishment I have read with attention the sentiments you have submitted to my perusal. — Be assured Sir, no occurrence in the course of the War, has given me more painful sensations than your information of there being such ideas existing in the Army as you have expressed, & I must view with abhorrence, and reprehend with severity — For the present, the communicatn. of them will rest in my own bosom, unless any further agitation of the matter, shall make a disclosure necessary. —

   I am much at a loss to conceive what part of my conduct could have given encouragement to an address which to me seems big with the greatest mischiefs that can befall my Country. — If I am not deceived in the knowledge of myself, you could not have found a person to whom your schemes are more disagreeable — At the same time in justice to my own feeling I must add, that no man possesses a more sincere wish to see ample justice done to the Army than I do, and as far as my powers & influence, in a constitutional way extend, they shall be employed to the utmost of my abilities to effect it, should there be any occasion — Let me conjure you then, if you have any regard for your Country, concern for yourself or posterity — or respect for me, to banish these thoughts from your Mind, & never communicate, as from yourself, or anyone else, a sentiment of the like Nature.

   With esteem I am Sir

Yr. Most Obed Ser
G. Washington

Col.º Nicola

THE TREATY OF PARIS, 1783

In the Treaty of Paris, concluded on September 3, 1783, Great Britain recognized the independence of the United States. Franklin, Adams, and Jay signed for the United States and Hartley for Great Britain. The original document is in the National Archives at Washington.

7

Original Definitive Treaty
3 Sept. 1783

Duplicate

In the Name of the most Holy & undivided Trinity.

It having pleased the devine Providence to dispose the Hearts of the most Serene and most Potent Prince George the third, by the Grace of God, King of Great Britain, France & Ireland, Defender of the Faith, Duke of Brunswick and Lunebourg, Arch Treasurer, and Prince Elector of the Holy Roman Empire &c°and of the United States of America to forget all past Misunderstandings and Differences that have unhappily interrupted the good Correspondence and Friendship which they mutually wish to restore; and to establish such a beneficial and satisfactory Intercourse between the two Countries upon the Ground of reciprocal Advantages and mutual Convenience as may promote and secure to both perpetual Peace & Harmony and having for this desirable End already laid the Foundation of Peace & Reconciliation by the Provisional Articles signed at Paris on the 30th of Novr. 1782. by the Commissioners empower'd on each Part, which Articles were agreed to be inserted in and to constitute the Treaty of Peace proposed to be concluded between the Crown of Great Britain and the said United States, but which Treaty was not to be concluded until Terms of Peace should be agreed upon between Great Britain & France, And his Britannic Majesty should be ready to conclude such Treaty accordingly: and the Treaty between Great Britain & France having since been concluded, His Britannic Majesty & the United States of America, in Order to carry into full Effect the Provisional Articles abovementioned, according to the Tenor thereof, have constituted & appointed, that is to say His Britannic Majesty on his Part, David Hartley Esqr, Member of the Parliament of Great Britain; and the said United States on their Part, John Adams Esqr, late a Commissioner of the United States of America at the Court of Versailles, late Delegate in Congress from the State of Massachusetts and Chief Justice of the said State, and Minister Plenipotentiary of the said United States to their High Mightinesses the States General of the United Netherlands; Benjamin Franklin Esqre late Delegate in Congress from the State of Pennsylvania, President of the Convention of the sd State, and Minister Plenipotentiary from the United States of America at the Court of Versailles,

John Jay Esqre late President of Congress, and Chief Justice of the State of New-York & Minister Plenipotentiary from the said United States at the Court of Madrid; to be the Plenipotentiaries for the concluding and signing the Present Definitive Treaty; who after having reciprocally communicated their respective full Powers have agreed upon and confirmed the following Articles.

ARTICLE 1st

His Britannic Majesty acknowledges the sd United States, viz. New-Hampshire Massachusetts Bay, Rhode-Island & Providence Plantations, Connecticut, New York, New Jersey, Pennsylvania, Delaware, Maryland, Virginia, North Carolina, South Carolina & Georgia, to be free sovereign & Independent States; that he treats with them as such, and for himself his Heirs & Successors, relinquishes all Claims to the Government Propriety & Territorial Rights of the same & every Part thereof.

ARTICLE 2d

And that all Disputes which might arise in future on the Subject of the Boundaries of the said United States, may be prevented, it is hereby agree and declared, that the following are and shall be their Boundaries, Viz. From the North West Angle of Nova Scotia, viz. That Angle which is formed by a Line drawn due North from the Source of Saint Croix River to the Highlands along the said Highlands which divide those Rivers that empty themselves into the River St Lawrence, from those which fall into the Atlantic Ocean, to the Northwesternmost Head of Connecticut River: Thence down along the middle of that River to the forty fifth Degree of North Latitude; From thence by a Line due West on said Latitude until it strikes the River Iroquois or Cataraquy; Thence along the middle of said River into Lake Ontario; through the Middle of said Lake until it strikes the Communication by Water between that Lake & Lake Erie; Thence along the middle of said Communication into Lake Erie; through the middle of said Lake, until it arrives at the Water Communication between that Lake & Lake Huron; Thence along the middle of said Water-Communication into the Lake Huron, thence through the middle of said Lake to the

Water Communication between that Lake and Lake Superior, thence through Lake Superior Northward of the Isles Royal & Phelipeaux to the Long Lake; Thence through the Middle of said Long. Lake, and the Water Communication between it & the Lake of the Woods, to the said Lake of the Woods; Thence through the said Lake to the most North-western Point thereof, and from thence on a due West Course to the River Mississippi, Thence by a Line to be drawn along the Middle of the said River Mississippi until it shall intersect the Northernmost Part of the thirty first Degree of North Latitude. South, by a Line to be drawn due East from the Determination of the Line last mentioned, in the Latitude of thirty one Degrees North of the Equator to the middle of the River Apalachicola or Catahouche. Thence along the middle thereof to its Junction with the Flint River; Thence straight to the Head of St Mary's River, and thence down along the middle of St Mary's River to the Atlantic Ocean. East, by a Line to be drawn along the Middle of the River St Croix, from its Mouth in the Bay of Fundy to its Source; and from its Source directly North to the aforesaid Highlands, which divide the Rivers that fall into the Atlantic Ocean, from those which fall into the River St Lawrence; comprehending all Islands within twenty Leagues of any Part of the Shores of the United States, & lying between Lines to be drawn due East from the Points where the aforesaid Boundaries between Nova Scotia on the one Part and East Florida on the other, shall respectively touch the Bay of Fundy and the Atlantic Ocean, excepting such Islands as now are or heretofore have been within the Limits of the said Province of Nova Scotia.

ARTICLE 3d

It is agreed that the People of the United States shall continue to enjoy unmolested the Right to take Fish of every kind on the Grand Bank and on all the other Banks of New-foundland, also in the Gulph of St Lawrence, and at all other Places in the Sea where the Inhabitants of both Countries used at any time heretofore to fish. And also that the Inhabitants of the United States shall have Liberty to take Fish of every Kind on such Part of the Coast of New-foundland as British Fishermen shall use, (but not to dry or cure the same on that Island) And also on the Coasts Bays & Creeks of all other of his Britannic Majesty's Dominions in America, and that the American Fishermen shall have Liberty to dry and cure Fish in any of the Unsettled Bays Harbours and Creeks of Nova Scotia, Magdalen Islands, and Labrador, so long as the same shall remain unsettled but so soon as the same or either of them shall be settled, it shall not be lawful for the said Fishermen to dry or cure Fish at such Settlement, without a previous Agreement for that purpose with the Inhabitants, Proprietors or Possessors of the Ground.

ARTICLE 4th

It is agreed that Creditors on either Side shall meet with no lawful Impediment to the Recovery of the full Value in Sterling Money of all bona fide Debts heretofore contracted.

ARTICLE 5th

It is agreed that the Congress shall earnestly recommend it to the Legislatures of the respective States to provide for the Restitution of all Estates, Rights and Properties which have been confiscated belonging to real British Subjects; and also of the Estates Rights and Properties of Persons resident in Districts in the Possession of his Majesty's Arms, and who have not borne Arms against the said United States. And that Persons of any other Description shall have free Liberty to go to any Part or Parts of any of the thirteen United States and therein to remain twelve months unmolested in their Endeavours to obtain the Restitution of such of their Estates Rights & Properties as may have been confiscated. And that Congress shall also earnestly recommend to the several States, a Reconsideration and Revision of all Acts or Laws regarding the Premises, so as to render the said Laws or Acts perfectly consistent, not only with Justice and Equity, but with that Spirit of Conciliation, which, on the Return of the Blessings of Peace should universally prevail. And that Congress shall also earnestly recommend to the several States, that the Estates, Rights and Properties of such last mentioned Persons shall be restored to them, they refunding to any persons who may be now in Possession, the Bona fide Price (where any has been given) which such Persons may have paid on purchasing any of the said Lands, Rights or Properties since the Confiscation.

And it is agreed that all Persons who have any Interest in confiscated Lands, either by Debts, Marriage Settlements, or otherwise, shall meet with no lawful Impediment in the Prosecution of their just Rights.

ARTICLE 6th

That there shall be no future Confiscations made nor any Prosecutions commenc'd against any Person or Persons for or by Reason of the Part, which he or they may have taken in the present War, and that no Person shall on that Account suffer any future Loss or Damage, either in his Person Liberty or Property; and that those who may be in Confinement on such Charges at the Time of the Ratification of the Treaty in America shall be immediately set at Liberty, and the Prosecutions so commenced be discontinued.

ARTICLE 7th

There shall be a firm and perpetual Peace between his Britannic Majesty and the said States and between the Subjects of the one, and the Citizens of the other, wherefore all Hostilities both by Sea and Land shall from henceforth cease: All Prisoners on both Sides shall be set at Liberty, and his Britannic Majesty shall with all convenient speed, and without causing any Distruction, or carrying away any Negroes or other Property of the American Inhabitants, withdraw all his Armies, Garrisons & Fleets from the said United States, and from every Port, Place and Harbour within the same; leaving in all Fortifications the American Artillery that may be therein: And shall also Order & cause all Archives, Records, Deeds & Papers belonging to any of the said States, or their Citizens, which in the Course of the War may have fallen into the Hands of his Officers, to be forthwith restored and deliver'd to the proper States and Persons to whom they belong .

ARTICLE 8th

The Navigation of the River Mississippi, from its source to the Ocean shall for ever remain free and open to the Subjects of Great Britain and the Citizens of the United States.

ARTICLE 9th

In Case it should so happen that any Place or Territory belonging to great Britain or to the United States should have been conquer'd by the Arms of either from the other before the Arrival of the said Provisional Articles in America it is agreed that the same shall be restored without Difficulty and without requiring any Compensation.

ARTICLE 10th

The solemn Ratifications of the present Treaty expedited in good & due Form shall be exchanged between the contracting Parties in the Space of Six Months or sooner if possible to be computed from the Day of the Signature of the present Treaty. In Witness whereof we the undersigned their Ministers Plenipotentiary have in their Name and in Virtue of our Full Powers signed with our Hands the present Definitive Treaty, and caused the Seals of our Arms to be affix'd thereto.

Done at Paris, this third Day of September, In the Year of our Lord one thousand seven hundred & eighty three. ——————

D Hartley   John Adams.   B Franklin   John Jay

THE NORTHWEST ORDINANCE

A milestone in the development of the American way of life, the Northwest Ordinance was passed by the Congress of the Confederation on July 13, 1787. It not only provided for the government of the Northwest Territory and the extension to its inhabitants of such individual liberties as freedom of religion and trial by jury, but it set the pattern for the admission of States to the Union. The official printed text of the Ordinance, signed by Charles Thomson, Jr., Secretary of the Congress, is in the National Archives at Washington.

8

AN ORDINANCE for the GOVERNMENT of the TERRITORY of the UNITED STATES, North-West of the RIVER OHIO.

BE IT ORDAINED by the United States in Congress assembled, That the said territory, for the purposes of temporary government, be one district; subject, however, to be divided into two districts, as future circumstances may, in the opinion of Congress, make it expedient.

Be it ordained by the authority aforesaid, That the estates both of resident and non-resident proprietors in the said territory, dying intestate, shall descend to, and be distributed among their children, and the descendants of a deceased child in equal parts; the descendants of a deceased child or grand-child, to take the share of their deceased parent in equal parts among them: And where there shall be no children or descendants, then in equal parts to the next of kin, in equal degree; and among collaterals, the children of a deceased brother or sister of the intestate, shall have in equal parts among them their deceased parents share; and there shall in no case be a distinction between kindred of the whole and half blood; saving in all cases to the widow of the intestate, her third part of the real estate for life, and one third part of the personal estate; and this law relative to descents and dower, shall remain in full force until altered by the legislature of the district. —————— And until the governor and judges shall adopt laws as herein after mentioned, estates, in the said territory may be devised or bequeathed by wills in writing, signed and sealed by him or her, in whom the estate may be, (being of full age) and attested by three witnesses; — and real estates may be conveyed by lease and release, or bargain and sale, signed, sealed, and delivered by the person being of full age, in whom the estate may be, and attested by two witnesses, provided such wills be duly proved, and such conveyances be acknowledged, or the execution thereof duly proved, and be recorded within one year after proper magistrates, courts, and registers shall be-appointed for that purpose; and personal property may be transferred by delivery, saving, however, to the French and Canadian inhabitants, and other settlers of the Kaskaskies, Saint Vincent's, and the neighbouring villages, who have heretofore professed themselves citizens of Virginia, their laws and customs now in force among them, relative to the descent and conveyance of property.

Be it ordained by the authority aforesaid, That there shall be appointed from time to time, by Congress, a governor, whose commission shall continue in force for the term of three years, unless sooner revoked by Congress; he shall reside in the district, and have a freehold estate therein, in one thousand acres of land, while in the exercise of his office.

There shall be appointed from time to time, by Congress, a secretary, whose commission shall continue in force for four years, unless sooner revoked, he shall reside in the district, and have a freehold estate therein, in five hundred acres of land, while in the exercise of his office; it shall be his duty to keep and preserve the acts and laws passed by the legislature, and the public records of the district, and the proceedings of the governor in his executive department; and transmit authentic copies of such acts and proceedings, every six months, to the secretary of Congress: There shall also be appointed a court to consist of three judges, any two of whom to form a court, who shall have a common law jurisdiction, and reside in the district, and have each therein a freehold estate in five hundred acres of land, while in the exercise of their offices; and their commissions shall continue in force during good behaviour.

The governor and judges, or a majority of them, shall adopt and publish in the district, such laws of the original states, criminal and civil, as may be necessary, and best suited to the circumstances of the district, and report them to Congress, from time to time, which laws shall be in force in the district until the organization of the general assembly therein, unless disapproved of by Congress; but afterwards the legislature shall have authority to alter them as they shall think fit.

The governor for the time being, shall be commander in chief of the militia, appoint and commission all officers in the same, below the rank of general officers; all general officers shall be appointed and commissioned by Congress.

Previous to the organization of the general assembly, the governor shall appoint such magistrates and other civil officers, in each county or township, as he shall find necessary for the preservation of the peace and good order in the same: After the general assembly shall be organized, the powers and duties of magistrates and other civil officers shall be regulated and defined by the said assembly; but all magistrates and other civil officers, not herein otherwise directed, shall, during the continuance of this temporary government, be appointed by the governor.

For the prevention of crimes and injuries, the laws to be adopted or made shall have force in all parts of the district, and for the execution of process, criminal and civil, the governor shall make proper divisions thereof — and he shall proceed from time to time, as circumstances may require, to lay out the parts of the district in which the Indian titles shall have been extinguished, into counties and townships, subject, however, to such alterations as may thereafter be made by the legislature.

So soon as there shall be five thousand free male inhabitants, of full age, in the district, upon giving proof thereof to the governor, they shall receive authority, with time and place, to elect representatives from their counties or townships, to represent them in the general assembly; provided that for every five hundred free male inhabitants there shall be one representative, and so on progressively with the number of free male inhabitants, shall the right of representation increase, until the number of representatives shall amount to twenty-five, after which the number and proportion of representatives shall be regulated by the legislature; provided that no person be eligible or qualified to act as a representative, unless he shall have been a citizen of one of the United States three years and be a resident in the district, or unless he shall have resided in the district three years, and in either case shall likewise hold in his own right, in fee simple, two hundred acres of land within the same: — Provided also, that a freehold in fifty acres of land in the district, having been a citizen of one of the states, and being resident in the district; or the like freehold and two years residence in the district shall be necessary to qualify a man as an elector of a representative.

The representatives thus elected, shall serve for the term of two years, and in case of the death of a representative, or removal from office, the governor shall issue a writ to the county or township for which he was a member, to elect another in his stead, to serve for the residue of the term.

The general assembly, or legislature, shall consist of the governor, legislative council, and a house of representatives. The legislative council shall consist of five members, to continue in office five years, unless sooner removed by Congress, and three of whom to be a quorum, and the members of the council shall be nominated and appointed in the following manner, to wit: As soon as representatives shall be elected, the governor shall appoint a time and place for them to meet together, and, when met, they shall nominate ten persons, residents in the district, and each possessed of a freehold in five hundred acres of land, and return their names to Congress; five of whom Congress shall appoint and commission to serve as aforesaid; and, whenever a vacancy shall happen in the council, by death or removal from office, the house of representatives shall nominate two persons, qualified as aforesaid, for each vacancy, and return their names to Congress; one of whom Congress shall appoint and commission for the residue of the term; and every five years, four months at least before the expiration of the time of service of the members of council, the said house shall nominate ten persons, qualified as aforesaid, and return their names to Congress, five of whom Congress shall appoint and commission to serve as members of the council five years, unless sooner removed. And the governor, legislative council, and house of representatives, shall have authority to make laws in all cases for the good government of the district, not repugnant to the principles and articles in this ordinance established and declared. And all bills having passed by a majority in the house, and by majority in the council, shall be referred to the governor for his assent; but no bill or legislative act whatever, shall be of any force without his assent. The governor shall have power to convene, prorogue and dissolve the general assembly, when in his opinion it shall be expedient.

The governor, judges, legislative council, secretary, and such other officers as Congress shall appoint in the district, shall take an oath or affirmation of fidelity, and of office, the governor before the president of Congress, and all other officers before the governor. As soon as a legislature shall be formed in the district, the council and house, assembled in one room, shall have authority by joint ballot to elect a delegate to Congress, who shall have a seat in Congress, with a right of debating, but not of voting, during this temporary government.

And for extending the fundamental principles of civil and religious liberty, which form the basis whereon these republics, their laws and constitutions are erected; to fix and establish those principles as the basis of all laws, constitutions and governments, which forever hereafter shall be formed in the said territory; — to provide also for the establishment of states, and permanent government therein, and for their admission to a share in the federal councils on an equal footing with the original states, at as early periods as may be consistent with the general interest:

It is hereby ordained and declared by the authority aforesaid, That the following articles shall be considered as articles of compact between the original states and the people and states in the said territory, and forever remain unalterable, unless by common consent, to wit:

Article the first. No person, demeaning himself in a peacable and orderly manner, shall ever be molested on account of his mode of worship or religious sentiments in the said territory.

Article the second. The inhabitants of the said territory shall always be entitled to the benefits of the writ of habeas corpus, and of the trial by jury; of a proportionate representation of the people in the legislature, and of judicial proceedings according to the course of the common law; all persons shall be bailable unless for capital offences, where the proof shall be evident, or the presumption great; all fines shall be moderate, and no cruel or unusual punishments shall be inflicted; no man shall be deprived of his liberty or property but by the judgment of his peers, or the law of the land; and should the public exigencies make it necessary for the common preservation to take any person's property, or to demand his particular services, full compensations shall be made for the same; — and in the just preservation of rights and property it is understood and declared, that no law ought ever to be made, or have force in the said territory, that shall in any manner whatever interfere with, or affect private contracts or engagements, bona fide and without fraud previously formed.

Article the third. Religion, morality and knowledge, being necessary to good government and the happiness of mankind, schools and the means of education shall forever be encouraged. The utmost good faith shall always be observed towards the Indians; their lands and property shall never be taken from them without their consent; and in their property, rights and liberty, they never shall be invaded or disturbed, unless in just and lawful wars authorized by Congress; but laws founded in justice and humanity shall from time to time be made, for preventing wrongs being done to them; and for preserving peace and friendship with them.

Article the fourth. The said territory, and the states which may be formed therein, shall forever remain a part of this confederacy of the United States of America, subject to the articles of confederation, and to such alterations therein as shall be constitutionally made; and to all the acts and ordinances of the United states in Congress assembled, conformable thereto. The inhabitants and settlers in the said territory, shall be subject to pay a part of the federal debts contracted or to be contracted, and a proportional part of the expences of government, to be apportioned on them by Congress, according to the same common rule and measure by which apportionments thereof shall be made on the other states; and the taxes for paying their proportion, shall be laid and levied by the authority and direction of the legislatures of the district or districts or new states, as in the original states, within the time agreed upon by the United States in Congress assembled. The legislatures of those districts, or new states, shall never interfere with the primary disposal of the soil by the United States in Congress assembled, nor with any regulations Congress may find necessary for securing the title in such soil to the bona fide purchasers. No tax shall be imposed on lands the property of the United States; and in no case shall non-resident proprietors be taxed higher than residents. The navigable waters leading into the Mississippi and St. Lawrence, and the carrying places between the same shall be common highways, and forever free, as well to the inhabitants of the said territory, as to the citizens of the United States, and those of any other states that may be admitted into the confederacy, without any tax, impost or duty therefor.

Article the fifth. There shall be formed in the said territory, not less than three nor more than five states; and the boundaries of the states, as soon as Virginia shall alter her act of cession and consent to same, shall become fixed and established as follows, to wit: The western state in the said territory, shall be bounded by the Mississippi, the Ohio and Wabash rivers; a direct line drawn from the Wabash and Post Vincent's due north to the territorial line between the United States and Canada, and by the said territorial line to the lake of the Woods and Mississippi. The middle state shall be bounded by the said direct line, the Wabash from Post Vincent's to the Ohio; by the Ohio, by a direct line drawn due north from the mouth of the Great Miami to the said territorial line, and by the said territorial line. The eastern state shall be bounded by the last mentioned direct line, the Ohio, Pennsylvania, and the said territorial line; Provided however, and it is further understood and declared, that the boundaries of these three states, shall be subject so far to be altered, that if Congress shall hereafter find it expedient, they shall have authority to form one or two states in that part of the said territory which lies north of an east and west line drawn through the southerly bend or extreme of lake Michigan: and whenever any of the said states shall have sixty thousand free inhabitants therein, such state shall be admitted by its delegates into the Congress of the United states, on an equal footing with the original states in all respects whatever; and shall be at liberty to form a permanent constitution and state government: Provided the constitution and government so to be formed, shall be republican, and in conformity to the principles contained in these articles; and so far as it can be consistent with the general interest of the confederacy, such admission shall be allowed at an earlier period, and when there may be a less number of free inhabitants in the state than sixty thousand.

Article the sixth. There shall be neither slavery nor involuntary servitude in the said territory, otherwise than in punishment of crimes whereof the party shall have been duly convicted: Provided always, that any person escaping into the same, from whom labor or service is lawfully claimed in any one of the original states, such fugitive may be lawfully reclaimed and conveyed to the person claiming his or her labor or service as aforesaid.

Be it ordained by the authority aforesaid, That the resolutions of the 23d of April, 1784, relative to the subject of this ordinance, be, and the same are hereby repealed and declared null and void.

DONE by the UNITED STATES in CONGRESS assembled, the 13th day of July, in the year of our Lord 1787, and of their sovereignty and independence the 12th.

*Cha*ˢ*. Thomson, Jur*

WASHINGTON'S COPY OF THE CONSTITUTION

This printed draft of the Constitution as it was presented to the Convention by the Committee of Detail in August, 1787 belonged to George Washington, who was President of the Constitutional Convention. The corrections are in his handwriting and are reproduced below in italics. The original document, the first page of which is reproduced here, is in the National Archives at Washington.

9

WE the People of the States of New-Hampshire, Massachusetts, Rhode-Island and Providence Plantations, Connecticut, New-York, New-Jersey, Pennsylvania, Delaware, Maryland, Virginia, North-Carolina, South-Carolina, and Georgia, do ordain, declare and establish the following Constitution for the Government of Ourselves and our Posterity.

ARTICLE I.

The stile of this Government shall be, "The United States of America."

II.

The Government shall consist of supreme legislative, executive and judicial powers.

III.

The legislative power shall be vested in a Congress, to consist of two separate and distinct bodies of men, a House (1) of Representatives, and a Senate; ~~each of which shall, in all* cases, have a negative on the other. The Legislature shall meet on the first Monday in December in every year.~~

IV.

Sect. 1. The Members of the House of Representatives shall be chosen every second year, by the people of the several States comprehended within this Union. The qualifications of the electors shall be the same, from time to time, as those of the electors in the several States, of the most numerours branch of their own legislatures.

Sect. 2. Every Member of the House of Representatives shall be of the age of twenty-five years at least; shall have been a citizen of the United States for at least *seven* years before his election; and shall be, at the time of his election, *an inhabitant* of the State in which he shall be chosen.

Sect. 3. The House of Representatives shall, at its first formation, and until the number of citizens and inhabitants shall be taken in the manner herein after described, consist of sixty-five Members, of whom three shall be chosen in New-Hampshire, eight in Massachusetts, one in Rhode-Island and Providence Plantations, five in Connecticut, six in New-York, four in New-Jersey, eight in Pennsylvania, one in Delaware, six in Maryland, ten in Virginia, five in North-Carolina, five in South-Carolina, and three in Georgia.

Sect. 4. As the proportions of numbers in the different States will alter from time to time; as some of the States may hereafter be divided; as others may be enlarged by addition of territory; as two or more States may be united; as new States will be erected within the limits of the United States, the Legislature shall, in each of these cases, regulate the number of representatives by the number of inhabitants, according to *the rate hereinafter* (illegible) *not exceeding* the rate of one for every forty thousand. *Provided that every State shall have at least one representative.*

Sect. 5. All bills for raising or appropriating money, and for fixing the salaries of the officers of government, shall originate in the House of Representatives, and shall not be altered or amended by the Senate. No money shall be drawn from the public Treasury, but in pursuance of appropriations that shall originate in the House of Representatives.

Sect. 6. The House of Representatives shall have the sole power of impeachment. It shall choose its Speaker and other officers.

Sect. 7. Vacancies in the House of Representatives shall be supplied by writs of election from the executive authority of the State, in the representation from which they shall happen.   V.

(1) (in the left margin of Article 3)

The Legislature shall meet at least once in every year and that meeting shall be on the first Monday in December unless a different day shall be appointed by Law.

(2) (in the left margin of Section 5)

Line (illegible) be reconsidered & struck out

WASHINGTON'S FIRST INAUGURAL ADDRESS

In this brief address, written in his own hand, the first president of the United States speaks modestly of his qualifications for office and states his conviction that "the preservation of the sacred fire of liberty and the destiny of the republican model of government are . . . intrusted to the hands of the American people." The original is in the National Archives at Washington.

10

Fellow Citizens of the Senate
and
of the House of Representatives.

Among the vicissitudes incident to life, no event could have filled me with greater anxieties than that of which the notification was transmitted by your order, and received on the fourteenth day of the present month:————— On the one hand, I was summoned by my Country, whose voice I can never hear but with veneration and love, from a retreat which I had chosen with the fondest predilection, and, in my flattering hopes, with an immutable decision, as the asylum of my declining years: a retreat which was rendered every day more necessary as well as more dear to me, by the addition of habit to inclination, and of frequent interruptions in my health to the gradual waste committed on it by time. ————— On the other hand, the magnitude and difficulty of the trust to which the voice of my Country called me, being sufficient to awaken in the wisest and most experienced of her citizens, a distrustful scrutiny into his qualifications, could not but overwhelm with dispondence, one, who, inheriting inferior endowments from nature and unpractised in the duties of civil administration, ought to be peculiarly conscious of his own deficiencies. —————
In this conflict of emotions, all I dare aver, is, that it has been my faithful study to collect my duty from a just appreciation of every circumstance, by which it might be affected. ————— All I dare hope, is, that, if in executing this task I have been too much swayed by a grateful remembrance of former instances, or by an affectionate sensibility to this transcendent proof, of the confidence of my fellow-citizens; and have thence too little consulted my incapacity as well as disinclination for the weighty and untried cares before me; my error will be palliated by the motives which misled me, and its consequences be judged by my Country, with some share of the partiality in which they originated. —————

Such being the impressions under which I have, in obedience to the public summons, repaired to the present station; it would be peculiarly improper to omit in this first official Act, my fervent supplications to that Almighty Being who rules over the Universe, ————— Who presides in the Councils of Nations, ————— and whose

providential aids can supply every human defect, that his benediction may consecrate to the liberties and happiness of the People of the United States, a Government instituted by themselves for these essential purposes: and may enable every instrument employed in its administration to execute with success, the functions allotted to his charge. ————— In tendering this homage to the Great Author of every public and private good, I assure myself that it expressed your sentiments not less than my own; ————— nor those of my fellow-citizens at large, less than either. —————
————— No People can be bound to acknowledge and adore the invisible hand, which conducts the Affairs of men more than the People of the United States. ————— Every step, by which they have advanced to the character of an independent nation, seems to have been distinguished by some token of providential agency. ————— And in the important revolution just accomplished in the system of their United Government; the tranquil deliberations and voluntary consent of so many distinct communities, from which the event has

resulted, cannot be compared with the means by which most Governments have been established, without some return of pious gratitude along with an humble anticipation of the future blessings which the past seem to presage. —————————— These reflections, arising out of the present crisis, have forced themselves too strongly on my mind to be suppressed. —————————— You will join with me I trust in thinking, that there are none under the influence of which, the proceedings of a new and free Government can more auspiciously commence. —————————

By the article establishing the Executive Department, it is made the duty of the President "to recommend to your consideration, such measures as he shall Judge necessary and expedient." —————————— The circumstances under which I now meet you, will acquit me from entering into that subject, farther than to refer to the Great Constitutional Charter under which you are assembled; and which, in defining your powers, designates the objects to which your attention is to be given. —————————— It will be more consistent with those circumstances, and far more congenial with the feelings which actuate me, to substitute, in place of a recommendation of particular measures, the tribute that is due to the talents, the rectitude, and the patriotism which adorn the characters selected to devise and adopt them. ————— ————— In these honorable qualifications, I behold the surest pledges, that as on one side, no local prejudices, or attachments; no separate views, nor party animosities, will misdirect the comprehensive and equal eye which ought to watch over this great assemblage of communities and interests: so, on another, that the foundations of our National policy will be laid in the pure and immutable principles of private morality; and the pre-eminence of free Government, be exemplified by all attributes which can win the affections of its Citizens, and command the respect of the world. ————— ————— I dwell on this prospect with every satisfaction which an ardent love for my Country can inspire: since there is no truth more thoroughly established, than that there exists in the oeconomy and course of nature, an indissoluble union between virtue and happiness, —————————— between duty and advantage, —————————— between the genuine maxims of an honest and magnanimous policy, and the solid rewards of public prosperity and felicity: —————————— Since we ought to be no less persuaded that the propitious smiles of Heaven, can never be expected on a nation that disregards the eternal rules of order and right, which Heaven itself has ordained: —————————— And since the preservation of the sacred fire of liberty, and the destiny of the Republican model of Government, are justly considered as deeply, perhaps as finally staked, on the experiment entrusted to the hand of the American people.

Besides the ordinary objects submitted to your care, it will remain with your judgement to decide, how far an exercise of the occasional power delegated by the Fifth article of the Constitution is rendered expedient at the present juncture by the nature of objections which have been urged against the System, or by the degree of inquietude which has given birth to them.

Instead of undertaking particular recommendations on this subject, in which I could be guided by no lights derived from official opportunities, I shall again give way to my entire confidence in your discernment and pursuit of the public good: —————————— For I assure myself that whilst you carefully avoid every alteration which might endanger the benefits of an United and effective Government, or which ought to await the future lessons of experience; a reverence for the characteristic rights of freemen, and a regard for the public harmony, will sufficiently influence your deliberations on the question how far the former can be more impregnably fortified, or the latter be safely and advantageously premoted. —————————

To the preceding observations I have one to add, which will be most properly addressed to the House of Representatives.——————————It concerns myself, and will therefore be as brief as possible. —————————— When I was first honoured with a call into the Service of my Country, then on the eve of an arduous struggle for its liberties, the light in which I contemplated my duty required that I should renounce every pecuniary compensation. —————————— From this resolution I have in no instance departed. And being still under the impressions which produced it, I must decline as inapplicable to myself, any share in the personal emoluments, which may be indispensably included in a permanent provision for the Executive Department; and must accordingly pray that the pecuniary estimates for the Station in which I am placed, may, during my continuance in it, be limited to such actual expenditures as the public good may be thought to require. —————————

Having thus imparted to you my sentiments, as they have been awakened by the occasion which brings us together, —————————— I shall take my present leave; —————————— but not without resorting once more to the benign parent of the human race, in humble supplication that since he has been pleased to favor the American people, with opportunities for deliberating in perfect tranquility, and dispositions for deciding with unparellelled unanimity on a form of Government, for the security of their Union, and the advancement of their happiness,: so his divine blessing may be equally conspicuous in the enlarged views, ————— ————— The temperate consultations, —————————— and the wise measures on which the success of this Government must depend. —————————

G Washington

BILL OF RIGHTS

On September 25, 1789, the Congress proposed twelve articles of amendment to the Constitution of the United States. Except for the first two, they were ratified by the required number of states by December 15, 1791, and thus became the first ten amendments. They have since been known as the Bill of Rights. The enrolled original of the Congressional resolution is in the National Archives at Washington.

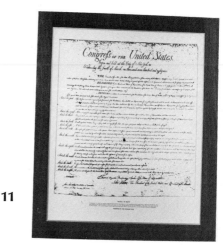

11

CONGRESS of the UNITED STATES
begun and held at the City of New-York, on Wednesday the fourth of March, one thousand seven hundred and eighty nine.

THE Conventions of a number of the States, having at the time of their adopting the Constitution, expressed a desire in order to prevent misconstruction or abuse of its powers, that further declaratory and restrictive clauses should be added: And as extending the ground of public confidence in the Government, will best insure the beneficent ends of its institutions.

RESOLVED by the Senate and House of Representatives of the United States of America in Congress assembled, two thirds of both Houses concurring, that the following Articles be proposed to the Legislatures of the several States as amendments to the Constitution of the United States, all, or any of which Articles, when ratified by three fourths of the said Legislatures, to be valid to all intents and purposes, as part of the said Constitution; viz.[6]

ARTICLES in addition to, and amendment of the Constitution of the United States of America, proposed by Congress, and ratified by the Legislatures of the several States, pursuant to the fifth Article of the original Constitution.

Article the first ...

After the first enumeration required by the first Article of the Constitution, there shall be one Representative for every thirty thousand, until the number shall amount to one hundred, after which, the proportion shall be so regulated by Congress, that there shall be not less than one hundred Representatives, nor less than one Representative for every forty thousand persons, until the number of Representatives shall amount to two hundred, after which the proportion shall be so regulated by Congress, that there shall not be less than two hundred Representatives, nor more than one Representative for every fifty thousand persons.

Article the second ...

No law, varying the compensation for the services of the Senators and Representatives, shall take effect, until an election of Representatives shall have intervened.

Article the third ...

Congress shall make no law respecting an estab-lishment of religion, or prohibiting the free exercise thereof; or abridging the freedom of speech, or of the press; or the right of the people peaceably to assemble, and to petition the Government for a redress of grievances.

Article the fourth ...

A Well regulated Militia, being necessary to the security of a free State, the right of the people to keep and bear Arms, shall not be infringed.

Article the fifth ...

No Soldier shall, in time of peace be quartered in any house, without the consent of the Owner, nor in time of war, but in a manner to be prescribed by law.

Article the sixth ...

The right of the people to be secure in their persons, houses, papers, and effects, against unreasonable searches and seizures, shall not be violated, and no Warrants shall issue, but upon probable cause, supported by Oath or affirmation, and particularly describing the place to be searched, and the persons or things to be seized.

Article the seventh ...

No person shall be held to answer for a capital, or otherwise infamous crime, unless on a presentment or indictment of a Grand Jury, except in cases arising in the land or naval forces, or in the Militia, when in actual service in time of War or public danger; nor shall any person be subject for the same offence to be twice put in jeopardy of life or limb; nor shall be compelled in any Criminal case to be a witness against himself, nor be deprived of life, liberty, or property, without due process of law; nor shall private property be taken for public use, without just compensation.

Article the eighth ...

In all criminal prosecutions, the accused shall enjoy the right to a speedy and public trial, by an impartial jury of the State and district wherein the crime shall have been committed, which district shall have been previously ascertained by law, and to be informed of the nature and cause of the accusation; to be confronted with the witnesses against him; to have compulsory process for obtaining Witnesses in his favor, and to have the Assistance of Counsel for his defence.

Article the ninth . . .

In suits at common law, where the value in controversy shall exceed twenty dollars, the right of trial by jury shall be preserved, and no fact tried by a jury shall be otherwise re-examined in any Court of the United States, than according to the rules of the common law.

Article the tenth . . .

Excessive bail shall not be required, nor excessive fines imposed, nor cruel and unusual punishments inflicted.

Article the eleventh . . .

The enumeration in the Constitution, of certain rights, shall not be construed to deny or disparage others retained by the people.

Article the twelfth . . .

The powers not delegated to the United States, by the Constitution, nor prohibited by it to the States, are reserved to the States respectively or to the people.

Frederick Augustus Muhlenberg
   Speaker of the House of Representatives.

ATTEST, *John Adams,*
   Vice-President of the United States,
   and President of the Senate.

John Beckley,
   Clerk of the House of Representatives.

Sam A. Otis
   Secretary of the Senate.

WASHINGTON'S FAREWELL ADDRESS — FIRST DRAFT

*Washington counseled his countrymen on the future of their foreign and domestic affairs in this memorable address which has exerted strong influence on the nation's political thought and the policies of its government ever since. When Washington seriously considered retirement from the Presidency at the end of his first term, he wrote his thoughts for a farewell message to James Madison on May 20, 1792. The message, together with Madison's answer, was put aside when the President was persuaded to seek another term.
In 1796, toward the end of his second term, using Madison's notes, he prepared this first draft, pages 3, 9, 10, and 19 of which are reproduced in the Freedom Shrine. The address finally published was one considerably altered and polished by Washington in collaboration with Alexander Hamilton and John Jay.*

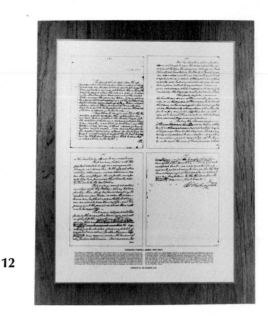

12

May 15, 1796

Friends and Fellow Citizens:

The quotation in this address was composed, and intended to have been published, in the year 1792; in time to have announced to the Electors of the President and Vice President of the United States, the determination of the former previous to the sd Election but the solicitude of my confidential friends added to the peculiar situation of our foreign affairs at that epoch induced me to suspend the promulgation; lest among other reasons my retirement might be ascribed to political cowardice. In place thereof I resolved, if it should be the pleasure of my fellow citizens to honor me again with their suffrages, to devote such services as I could render, a year or two longer; trusting that within that period all impediments to an honorable retreat would be removed.

In this hope, as fondly entertained as it was conceived, I entered upon the execution of the duties of my second administration. But if the causes wch produced this postponement had any weight in them at that period it will readily be acknowledged that there has been no diminution in them since, until very lately, and it will serve to account for the delay wch has taken place in communicating the sentiments which were then committed to writing, and are now found in the following words.

"The period which will close the appointment with which my fellow citizens have honoured me, being not very distant, and the time actually arrived, at which their thoughts must be designating the citizen who is to administer the Executive Government of the United States during the ensuing term, it may conduce to a more distinct expression of the public voice, that I should apprize such of my fellow citizen's as may retain their partiality towards me, that I am not to be numbered among those out of whom a choice is to be made." —

"I beg them to be assured that the Resolution which dictates this intimation has not been taken without the strictest regard to the relation which as a dutiful citizen I bear to my country; and that in withdrawing that tender of my service, which silence in my situation might imply, I am not influenced by the smallest deficiency of zeal for its future interests, or of grateful respect for its past kindness: but by the fullest persuasion that such a step is compatible with both."

The impressions under which I entered on the present arduous trust were explained on the proper occasion. In discharge of this trust, I can only say that I have contributed towards the organization and administration of the Government the best exertions of which a very fallible judgment was capable. For any errors which may have flowed from this source, I feel all the regret which an anxiety for the public good can excite; not without the double consolation, however, arising from a consciousness of their being involuntary, and an experience of the candor which will interpret them. If there were any circumstances which could give value to my inferior qualifications for the trust, these circumstances must have been temporary. In this light was the undertaking viewed when I ventured on it. Being, moreover still further advanced into the decline of life, I am every day more sensible that the increasing weight of years, renders the private walks of it in the shade of retirement, as necessary as they will be acceptable to me. May I be allowed to add, that it will be among the highest as well as the purest enjoyments that can sweeten the remnant of my days, to partake in a private station, in the midst of my fellow citizens, of that benign influence of good laws under a free Government, which has been the ultimate object of all my wishes, and in wch I confide as the happy reward of our cares and labours. [May I be allowed further to add as a consideration far more important, that an early example of rotation in an office of so high and delicate a nature, may equally accord with the republican spirit of our Constitution, and the ideas of liberty and safety entertained by the people.]

In contemplating the moment at which the curtain is to drop forever on the public scenes of my life, my sensations anticipate and do not permit me to suspend, the deep acknowledgments required by that debt of gratitude which I owe to my beloved country for the many honors it has conferred on me, for the distinguished confidence it has reposed in me, and for the opportunities I have thus enjoyed of testifying my inviolable attachment by the most steadfast services which my faculties could render. All the returns I have now to make will be in those vows which I shall carry with me to my retirement and to my grave, that Heaven may continue to favor the people of the United States with the choicest tokens of its beneficence; that their union and brotherly affection may be perpetual; that the free Constitution which is the work of their own hands, may be sacredly maintained; that its administration in every department, may be stamped with wisdom and with virtue; and that this character may be ensured to it, by that watchfulness over public servants and public measures, which on the one hand will be necessary, to prevent or correct a degeneracy; and that forbearance, on the other, from unfounded or indiscriminate jealousies which would deprive the public of the best services, by depriving a conscious integrity of one of the noblest incitements to perform them; that in fine the happiness of the people of America, under the auspices of liberty, may be made compleat, by so careful a preservation, and so prudent a use of this blessing, as will acquire them the glorious satisfaction of recommending it to the affection; the praise; and the adoption of every Nation which is yet a stranger to it.

And may we not dwell with well grounded hopes on this flattering prospect; when we reflect on the many ties by which the people of America are bound together, and the many proofs they have given of an enlightened judgment and a magnanimous patriotism.

We may all be considered as the Children of one common Country. We have all been embarked in one common cause. We have all had our share in common sufferings and common successes. The portion of the Earth allotted for the theatre of our fortunes, fulfils our most sanguine desires. All its essential interests are the same; while the diversities arising from climate, from soil, and from other local and lesser peculiarities, will naturally form a mutual relation of the parts, that may give the whole a more entire independence than has perhaps fallen to the lot of any other nation.

To confirm these motives to an affectionate and permanent Union, and to secure the great objects of it, we have established a common Government, which being free in its principles; being founded in our own choice; being intended as the guardian of our common rights; and the patron of our common interests; and wisely containing within itself a provision for its own amendment, as experience may point out its errors, seems to promise every thing that can be expected from such an institution; [and if supported by wise Councils, by virtuous conduct, and by mutual and friendly allowances, must approach as near to perfection as any human work can aspire, and nearer than any which the annals of mankind have recorded.]

With these wishes and hopes I shall make my exist [sic] from civil life; and I have taken the same liberty of expressing them, which I formerly used in offering the sentiments which were suggested by my exit from military life. If, in either instance, I have presumed more than I ought, on the indulgence of my fellow citizens, they will be too generous to ascribe it to any other cause, than the extreme solicitude which I am bound to feel, and which I can never cease to feel for their liberty, their prosperity, and their happiness."

Had the situation of our public affairs continued to wear the same aspect they assumed at the time the aforegoing address was drawn I should not have taken the liberty of troubling you — my fellow citizens — with any new sentiment or with a repition [sic for repetition] more in detail, of those which are therein contained; but considerable changes having taken place both at home & abroad, I shall ask your indulgence while I express with more lively sensibility, the following most ardent wishes of my heart

That party disputes, among all the friends and lovers of their country may subside, or, as the wisdom of Providence hath ordained that men, on the same subjects, shall not always think alike; that charity & benevolence when they happen to differ may so far shed their benign influence as to banish those invectives which proceed from illiberal prejudices and jealousy. —

That as the Allwise dispensor of human blessings has favored no Nation of the Earth with more abundant, & substantial means of happiness than United America, that we may not be so ungrateful to our Creator — so wanting to ourselves — and so regardless of Posterity — as to dash the cup of benificence which is thus bountifully offered to our acceptance.

That we may fulfil with the greatest exactitude all our engagements: foreign and domestic, to the utmost of our abilities whensoever, and in whatsoever manner they are pledged: for in public, as in private life, I am persuaded that honesty will forever be found to be the best policy

That we may avoid connecting ourselves with the Politics of any Nation, farther than shall be found necessary to regulate our own trade; in order that commerce may be placed upon a stable footing — our merchants know their rights — and the government the ground on which those rights are to be supported. —

That every citizen would take pride in the name of an American, and act as if he felt the importance of the character by considering that we ourselves are now a distinct Nation the dignity of which will be absorbed, if not annihilated, if we enlist ourselves (further than our obligations may require) under the banner of any other Nation whatsoever. — And moreover, that we would guard against the Intriegues of any and every foreign Nation who shall endeavor to intermingle (however covertly and indirectly) in the internal concerns of our country; or who shall attempt to prescribe rules for our policy with any other power, if there be no infraction of our engagements with themselves, as one of the greatest evils that can befal us as a people; for whatever may be their professions, be assured fellow Citizens and the event will (as it always has) invariably prove, that Nations as well as individuals, act for their own benefit, and not for the benefit of others, unless both interests happen to be assimilated (and when that is the case there requires no contract to bind them together). That all their interferences are calculated to promote the former; and in proportion as they succeed, will render us less independent. In a word, nothing is more certain than that, if we receive favors, we must grant favors; and it is not easy to decide beforehand under such circumstances as we are, on which side the balance will ultimately terminate; but easy indeed is it to foresee that it may involve us in disputes and finally in War, to fulfil political alliances. Whereas, if there be no engagements on our part, we shall be unembarrassed, and at liberty at all times, to act from circumstances, and the dictates of Justice, sound policy, and our essential Interests.

That we may be always prepared for War, but never unsheath the sword except in self defence so long as Justice and our essential rights, and national respectability can be preserved without it; for without the gift of prophecy, it may safely be pronounced, that if this country can remain in peace 20 years longer: and I devoutly pray that it may do so to the end of time; such in all probability will be its population, riches, and resources, when combined with its peculiarly happy and remote Situation from the other quarters of the globe, as to bid defiance, in a just cause, to any earthly power whatsoever.

That whensoever and so long as we profess to be Neutral, let our public conduct whatever our private affections may be, accord therewith; without suffering partialities on one hand, or prejudices on the other to controul our Actions. A contrary practice is not only incompatible with our declarations, but is pregnant with mischief, embarrassing to the Administration, tending to divide us into parties, and ultimately productive of all those evils and horrors which proceed from faction, and above all,

That our Union may be as lasting as time; for while we are encircled in one band, we shall possess the strength of a Giant and there will be none who can make us affraid. Divide, and we shall become weak; a prey to foreign Intriegues and internal discord; and shall be as miserable and contemptible as we are now enviable and happy. And lastly:

That the several departments of Government may be preserved in their utmost Constitutional purity, without any attempt of one to encroach on the rights or privileges of another; that the Genl and State governmts may move in their propr Orbits; And that the authorities of our own constituting may be respected by ourselves as the most certain means of having them respected by foreigners.

In expressing these sentiments it will readily be perceived that I can have no other view now, whatever malevolence might have ascribed to it before, than such as result from a perfect conviction of the utility of the measure. If public servants, in the exercise of their official duties are found incompetent or pursuing wrong courses discontinue them. If they are guilty of mal-practices in office, let them be more ex [em] plarily punished; in both cases the Constitution and Laws have made provision, but do not withdraw your confidence from them, the best incentive to a faithful discharge of their duty, without just cause; nor infer, because measures of a complicated nature, which time, opportunity and close investigation alone can penetrate, and for these reasons are not easily comprehended by those who do not possess the means, that it necessarily follows they must be wrong; This would not only be doing injustice to your Trustees, but be counteracting your own essential interests; rendering those Trustees (if not contemptible in the eyes of the world) little better at least than ciphers in the Administration of the government and the Constitution of your own chusing would reproach you for such conduct.

As this Address, Fellow citizens will be the last I shall ever make you, and as some of the Gazettes of the United States have teemed with all the Invective that disappointment, ignorance of facts, and malicious falsehoods could invent, to misrepresent my politics and affections; to wound my reputation and feelings; and to weaken, if not entirely destroy the confidence you had been pleased to repose in me; it might be expected at the parting scene of my public life that I should take some notice of such virulent abuse. But, as heretofore, I shall pass them over in utter silence; never having myself, nor by any other with my participation or knowledge, written, or published a scrap in answer to any of them. My politicks have been unconcealed; plain and direct. They will be found (so far as they relate to the Belligerent Powers) in the Proclamation of the 22d of April 1793; which, having met your approbation, and the confirmation of Congress, I have uniformly and steadily adhered to, uninfluenced by, and regardless of the complaints and attempts of any of those powers or their partisans to change them.

The Acts of my Administration are on Record. By these, which will not change with circumstances, nor admit of different interpretations, I expect to be judged. If they will not acquit me, in your estimation, it will be a source of regret; but I shall hope notwithstanding, as I did not seek the Office with which you have honored me, that charity may throw her mantle over my want of abilities to do better; that the gray hairs of a man who has, excepting the interval between the close of the Revolutionary War, and the organization of the new governmt. either in a civil, or military character, spent five and forty years, All the prime of his life, in serving his country, be suffered to pass quietly to the grave; and that his errors, however numerous; if they are not criminal, may be consigned to the Tomb of oblivion, as he himself soon will be to the Mansions of Retirement.

To err, is the lot of humanity, and never for a moment, have I ever had the presumption to suppose that I had not a full proportion of it. Infallibility not being the attribute of Man, we ought to be cautious in censuring the opinions and conduct of one another. To avoid intentional error in my public conduct, has been my constant endeavor; and I set malice at defiance to charge me, justly, with the commission of a wilful one; or, with the neglect of any public duty, which, in my opinion ought to have been performed, since I have been in the Administration of the government. An Administration which I do not hesitate to pronounce, the infancy of the government, and all other circumstances considered, that has been as delicate, difficult, and trying as may occur again in any future period of our history. Through the whole of which I have to the best of my judgment, and with the best information and advice I could obtain, consulted the true and permanent interest of my country without regard to local considerations, to individuals, to parties, or to Nations.

To conclude, and I feel proud in having it in my power to do so with truth, that it was not from ambitious views; it was not from ignorance of the hazard to which I know I was exposing my reputation; it was not from an expectation of pecuniary compensation, that I have yielded to the calls of my country; and that, if my country has derived no benefit from my services, my fortune, in a pecuniary point of view, has received no augmentation from my country. But in delivering this last sentiment, let me be unequivocally understood as not intending to express any discontent on my part, or to imply any reproach on my country on that account. [The first wd be untrue; the other ungrateful. And no occasion more fit than the present may ever occur perhaps to declare, as I now do declare, that nothing but the principle upon which I set out, and from which I have, in no instance departed, not to receive more from the public than my expences, has restrained the bounty of several Legislatures at the close of the War with Great Britain from adding considerably to my pecuniary resources.] I retire from the Chair of government no otherwise benefitted in this particular than what you have all experienced from the increased value of property, flowing from the Peace and prosperity with which our country has been blessed amidst tumults which have harrassed and involved other counties in all the horrors of War. — I leave you with undefiled hands — an uncorrupted heart — and with ardent vows to heaven for the welfare & happiness of that country in which I and my forefathers to the third or fourth Ancestry (progenitor) drew our first breath. —

Go. Washington

JEFFERSON'S FIRST INAUGURAL ADDRESS

13

Friends & fellow citizens

Called upon to undertake the duties of the first Executive office of our country, I avail myself of the presence of that portion of my fellow citizens which is here assembled to express my grateful thanks for the favor with which they have been pleased to look towards me, to declare a sincere consciousness that the task is above my talents, & that I approach it with those anxious & awful presentiments which the greatness of the charge & the weakness of my powers so justly inspire.

A rising nation spread over a wide and fruitful land, traversing all the seas with the rich productions of their industry, engaged in commerce with nations who feel power, and forget right, advancing rapidly to destinies beyond the reach of mortal eye. When I contemplate these transcendant objects, & see the honor the happiness, & the hopes of this beloved country committed to the issue & the auspices of this day, I shrink from the contemplation, & humble myself before the magnitude of the undertaking. Utterly indeed, should I despair, did not the presence of many whom I here see, remind me, that in the other high authorities provided by our Constitution, I shall find resources of wisdom of virtue, & of zeal on which to rely under all difficulties. To you then gentlemen who are charged with the sovereign functions of legislation & to those associated with you, I look with encouragement for that guidance & support which may enable us to steer with safety, the vessel in which we are all embarked amidst the conflicting elements of a troubled world.

During the contest of opinion through which we have passed, the animation of discussions and of exertions, has sometimes worn an aspect which might impose on strangers unused to think freely & to speak & to write what they think. But this being now decided by the voice of the nation anounced according to the rules of the constitution, all will of course arrange themselves under the will of the law, & unite in common efforts for the common good. All too well bear in mind this sacred principle, that though the will of the Majority is in all cases to prevail, that will, to be rightful, must be reasonable: That the Minority possess their equal rights, which equal laws must protect, & to violate would be oppression.

Let us then, fellow citizens, unite with one heart & one mind; let us restore to social intercourse that harmony and affection without which Liberty, & even life itself, are but dreary things. And let us reflect that having banished from our land that religious intolerance under which mankind so long bled & suffered, we have yet gained little, if we countenance a political intolerance as despotic, as wicked, & capable of as bitter & bloody persecution.

During the throes and convulsions of the antient world, during the agonizing spasms of infuriated man, seeking through blood & slaughter his long lost liberty, it was not wonderful that the agitation of the billows should reach even this distant & peaceful shore; that this should be more felt & feared by some, & less by others, & should divide opinions as to measures of safety. But every difference of opinion is not a difference of principle. We have called by different names, brethren of the same principle. We are all republicans: We are all federalists. If there be any among us who wish to dissolve this union, or to change it's republican form, let them stand undisturbed, as monuments of the safety with which error of opinion may be tolerated where reason is left free to combat it. I know indeed that some honest men have feared that a republican government cannot be strong; that this government is not strong enough. But would the honest patriot, in the full tide of successful experiment abandon a government which has so far kept us free & firm on the theoretic & visionary fear that this government, the world's best hope, may by possibility, want energy to preserve itself? I trust not. I believe this, on the contrary, the strongest government on earth. I believe it the only one where every man, at the call of the law, would fly to the standard of the law, & would meet invasions of public order, as

his own personal concern. Sometimes it is said that Man cannot be trusted with the government of himself.— Can he then be trusted with the government of others? Or have we found angels in the form of kings to govern him? — Let History answer this question.

Let us then, pursue with courage & confidence our own federal & republican principles, our attachment to Union, & Representative government, kindly separated by nature, & a wide ocean, from the exterminating havoc of one quarter of the globe, too high-minded to endure the degradations of the others; possessing a chosen country, with room enough for our descendants to the 1000th & 1000th generation; entertaining a due sense of our equal right, to the use of our own faculties, to the acquisitions of our own industry, to honor & confidence from our fellow citizens resulting not from birth, but from our actions & their sense of them, enlightened by a benign religion, professing indeed & practising in various forms, yet all of them inculcating Honesty, truth, temperance, gratitude, & the love of man, acknowledging & adoring an overruling providence, which by all its dispensations prooves that it delights in the happiness of man here, & his greater happiness hereafter: With all these blessings, what more is necessary to make us a happy and prosperous people? Still one thing more, fellow citizens, a wise & frugal government, which shall restrain men from injuring one another, shall leave them otherwise free to regulate their own pursuits of industry & improvement, and shall not take, from the mouth of labor, the bread it has earned. This is the sum of good government, & this is necessary to close the circle of our felicities.

About to enter, fellow-citizens, on the exercise of duties which comprehend everything dear and valuable to you, it is proper you should understand what I deem the essential principles of our Government, and consequently those which ought to shape its Administration. I will compress them within the narrowest compass they will bear, stating the general principle, but not all its limitations. Equal and exact justice to all men, of whatever state or persuasion, religious or political; peace, commerce, and honest friendship with all nations, entangling alliances with none; the support of the State governments in all their rights, as the most competent administrations for our domestic concerns and the surest bulwarks against antirepublican tendencies; the preservation of the General Government in its whole constitutional vigor, as the sheet anchor of our peace at home and safety abroad; a jealous care of the right of election by the people — a mild and safe corrective of abuses which are lopped by the sword of revolution where peaceable remedies are unprovided; absolute acquiescence in the decisions of the majority, the vital principle of republics, from which is no appeal but to force, the vital principle and

immediate parent of despotism; a well disciplined militia, our best reliance in peace and for the first moments of war, till regulars may relieve them; the supremacy of the civil over the military authority; economy in the public expense, that labor may be lightly burthened; the honest payment of our debts and sacred preservation of the public faith; encouragement of agriculture, and of commerce as its handmaid; the diffusion of information and arraignment of all abuses at the bar of the public reason; freedom of religion; freedom of the press, and freedom of person under the protection of the habeas corpus, and trial by juries impartially selected. These principles form the bright constellation which has gone before us and guided our steps through an age of revolution and reformation. The wisdom of our sages and blood of our heroes have been devoted to their attainment. They should be the creed of our political faith, the text of civic instruction, the touchstone by which to try the services of those we trust; and should we wander from them in moments of error or of alarm, let us hasten to retrace our steps and to regain the road which alone leads to peace, liberty, and safety.

I repair, then, fellow-citizens, to the post you have assigned me. With experience enough in subordinate offices to have seen the difficulties of this the greatest of all, I have learnt to expect that it will rarely fall to the lot of imperfect man to retire from this station with the reputation and the favor which bring him to it. Without pretensions to that high confidence you reposed in our first and greatest revolutionary character, whose preeminent services had entitled him to the first place in his country's love and destined for him the fairest page in the volume of faithful history, I ask so much confidence only as may give firmness and effect to the legal administration of your affairs. I shall often go wrong through defect of judgment. When right, I shall often be thought wrong by those whose positions will not command a view of the whole ground. I ask your indulgence for my own errors, which will never be intentional, and your support against the errors of others, who may condemn what they would not if seen in all its parts. The approbation implied by your suffrage is a great consolation to me for the past, and my future solicitude will be to retain the good opinion of those who have bestowed it in advance, to conciliate that of others by doing them all the good in my power, and to be instrumental to the happiness and freedom of all.

Relying, then, on the patronage of your good will, I advance with obedience to the work, ready to retire from it whenever you become sensible how much better choice it is in your power to make. And may that Infinite Power which rules the destinies of the universe lead our councils to what is best, and give them a favorable issue for your peace and prosperity.

"THE STAR SPANGLED BANNER"

After witnessing the unsuccessful British attack against Fort McHenry on September 13 and 14, 1814, Francis Scott Key wrote "The Star Spangled Banner," which in 1931 was made the national anthem by Act of Congress. The manuscript, in Key's writing, belongs to the Walters Art Gallery at Baltimore.

14

O say can you see, by the dawn's early light,
  What so proudly we hail'd at the twilight's
    last gleaming,
Whose broad stripes & bright stars through
    the perilous fight
  O'er the ramparts we watch'd, were so
    gallantly streaming?
    And the rocket's red glare, the bomb
      bursting in air,
    Gave proof through the night that our flag
      was still there,
O say does that star-spangled banner yet wave
O'er the land of the free & the home of
    the brave?

On the shore dimly seen through the mists
  of the deep,
  Where the foe's haughty host in dread
    silence reposes,
What is that which the breeze, o'er the
  towering steep,
As it fitfully blows, half conceals, half discloses?
  Now it catches the gleam of the morning's
    first beam,
  In full glory reflected now shines in the
    stream,
'Tis the star-spangled banner — O long
  may it wave
O'er the land of the free & the home of
    the brave!

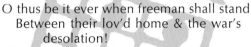

And where is that band who so vauntingly swore,
  That the havoc of war & the battle's confusion
A home & a Country should leave us no more?
  Their blood has wash'd out their foul
    footstep's pollution.
  No refuge could save the hireling & slave
From the terror of flight or the gloom
    of the grave,
And the star-spangled banner in triumph doth
  wave
  O'er the land of the free & the home of
    the brave.

O thus be it ever when freeman shall stand
  Between their lov'd home & the war's
    desolation!
Blest with vict'ry & peace may the heav'n
  rescued land
Praise the power that hath made &
    preserv'd us a nation!
  Then conquer we must, when our cause
    it is just,
  And this be our motto — "In God is our trust,"
And the star-spangled banner in triumph
  shall wave
  O'er the land of the free & the home of
    the brave.—

JACKSON'S LETTER DESCRIBING THE BATTLE OF NEW ORLEANS

Andrew Jackson, leader of the American forces in the decisive defeat of the British in the Battle of New Orleans, described the action and generously paid tribute to his men in a letter to the Secretary of War that was written and signed on January 9, 1815. The Treaty of Ghent, ending the War of 1812, had been signed in Europe on December 24, 1814, but this news had not yet reached the battlefield. The original letter is in the National Archives at Washington.

15

Camp 4 miles below Orleans
Sir: 9th Jan: 1815

During the days of the 6th. & 7th. the enemy had been actively employed in making preparations for an attack on my lines. With infinite labour they had succeeded on the night of the 7th in getting their boats across from the lake to the river, by widening & deepening the Canal on which they had effected their disembarkation. It had not been in my power to impede these operations by a general attack: Added to other reasons, the nature of the troops under my command, mostly militia, rendered it too hazardous to attempt extensive offensive movements in an open Country, against a numerous & well disciplined army.— Altho my forces, as to number, had been increased by the arrival of the Kentucky division—my strength had received very little addition; a small portion only of that detachment being provided with arms: Compelled thus to wait the attack of the enemy I took every measure to repele it when it whould be made, & to defeat the object he had in view. Genl. Morgan with the Orleans Contingent — the Louisiana Militia, & a strong detachment of the Kentucky troops occupy an entrenched Camp, on the opposite side of the river, protected by strong batteries on the bank erected & superintended by Commodore Patterson.

In my encampment every thing was ready for action, when early on the morning of the 8th. the enemy, after throwing a heavy shower of bombs & congreve rockets, advanced their columns on my right & left, to storm my entrenchments. I cannot speak sufficiently in praise of the firmness & deliberation with which my whole line received their approach:—more could not have been expected from veterans, inured to war. For an hour the fire of the small arms was as incessant & severe as can be imagined. The artillery too, directed by officers who displayed equal skill & courage did great execution— Yet the columns of the enemy continued to advance with a firmness which reflects upon them the greatest credit. Twice the column which approached me on my left was repulsed by the troops of Genl. Carrole — those of Genl. Coffee, & a division of the Kentucky Militia, & twice they formed again & renewed the assault.

At length however, cut to pieces, they fled in confusion from the feild, leaving it covered with their dead & wounded. The loss which the enemy sustained on this occasion cannot be estimated at less than 1500 in killed wounded & prisoners— Upwards of three hundred have already been delivered over for burial; & my men are still engaged in picking them up within my lines, & carrying them to the point where the enemy are to receive them. This is in addition to the dead & wounded whom the enemy have been enabled to carry from the feild during & since the action, & to those who have since died of the wounds they received. We have taken about 500 prisoners, upwards of 300 of whom are wounded: & a great part of them mortally. My loss has not exceeded, & I believe has not amounted to ten killed & as many wounded. The entire destruction of the enemy's army was now inevitable had it not been for an unfortunate occurence which at this moment, took place on the other side of the river. Simultaneously with his advance upon my lines, he had thrown over in his boats, a considerable force to the other side of the river. These having landed, were hardy enough to advance against the works of Genl. Morgan; & what is strange & difficult to account for, at the very moment when their entire discomfiture was looked for with a confidence approaching to certainty, the Kentucky reinforcements in whom so much reliance had been placed, ingloriously fled,—drawing after them, by their example, the remainder of the forces;—& thus, yielding to the enemy that most fortunate position. The batteries which had rendered me, for many days, the most important services—tho bravely defended were of course, now abandoned; not however until the guns had been spiked.

This unfortunate route had totally changed the aspect of affairs. The enemy now occupied a position from which they might annoy us without hazard, & by means of which they might have been enabled to defeat, in a great measure, the effects of our successes on this side the river. It became therefore an object of the first consequence to dislodge him as soon as possible. For this object all the means in my power, which I could with any safety use, were immediately put in preparation.

Perhaps however it was owing somewhat to another cause that I succeeded even beyond my expectations. In negotiating the terms of a temporary suspension of hosilities to enable the enemy to bury their dead; & provide for their wounded, I had required certain propositions to be aceeded to as a basis; among which this was one — that altho, hostilities should cease this side the river until 12 OCK of this day yet it was not to be understood that they should cease on the other side; but that no reinforcements should be sent across by either army until the expiration of that hour. His Excellency Majr Genl. Lambert beged time to consider of those propositions until 10 OCLK of to day; & in the meantime recrossed his troops. I need not tell you with how much eagerness I immediately regained possession of the position he had thus hastily quitted.

The enemy having concentered his forces may again attempt to drive me from my position by storm: Whenever he does: I have no doubt my men will act with their usual firmness, & sustain a character now become dear to them.

I have the honor to be
With great respect
Yr. Obt st
Andrew Jackson
Major Genl comdg

THE MONROE DOCTRINE

President James Monroe enunciated the famous Monroe Doctrine in his address to Congress of December 2, 1823. "The American continents, by the free and independent conditions which they have assumed and maintained, are henceforth not to be considered as subjects for future colonization by any European powers," and any attempt to interfere with them would be regarded as "the manifestation of an unfriendly disposition towards the United States," he said. The original manuscript is in the National Archives at Washington.

16

At the proposal of the Russian Imperial Government, made through the minister of the Emperor residing here, a full power and instructions have been transmitted to the minister of the United States at St. Petersburg, to arrange, by amicable negotiations, the respective rights and interests of the two nations on the northwest coast of this continent. A similar proposal has been made by his Imperial Majesty to the Government of Great Britain, which has likewise been acceded to. The Government of the United States has been desirous, by this friendly proceeding, of manifesting the great value which they have invariably attached to the friendship of the Emperor, and their solicitude to cultivate the best understanding with his Government. In the discussions to which this interest has given rise, and in the arrangements by which they may terminate, the occasion has been judged proper for asserting as a principle in which the rights and interests of the United States are involved, that the American continents, by the free and independent condition which they have assumed and maintain, are henceforth not to be considered as subjects for further colonization by any European powers . . .

It was stated at the commencement of the last session that a great effort was then making in Spain and Portugal to improve the condition of the people of those countries, and that it appeared to be conducted with extraordinary moderation. It need scarcely be remarked that the result has been, so far, very different from what was then anticipated. Of events in that quarter of the globe with which we have so much intercourse, and from which we derive our origin, we have always been anxious and interested spectators. The citizens of the United States cherish sentiments the most friendly in favor of the liberty and happiness of their fellow-men on that side of the Atlantic. In the wars of the European powers in matters relating to themselves we have never taken any part, nor does it comport with our policy so to do. It is only when our rights are invaded or seriously menaced that we resent injuries or make preparation for our defence. With the movements in this hemisphere we are, of necessity, more immediately connected, and by causes which must be obvious to all enlightened and impartial observers. The political system of the allied powers is essentially different in this respect from that of America. This difference proceeds from that, which exists in their respective — Governments, and to the defence of our own, which has been atchieved by the loss of so much blood and treasure, and matured by the wisdom of their most enlightened Citizens, and under which we have enjoyed unexampled felicity, this whole nation is devoted. We owe it therefore to candor, and to the amicable relations existing between the United States and those powers, to declare that we should consider any attempt on their part to extend their system to any portion of this Hemisphere, as dangerous to our peace and safety. With the existing Colonies or dependences of any European power, we have not interfered, and shall not interfere. But with the Governments who have declared their Independence, and maintained it, and whose Independence we have, on great consideration, and on just principles, acknowledged, we could not view any interposition for the purpose of oppressing them, or controling in any other manner, their destiny, by any European power, in any other light, than as the manifestation of an unfriendly disposition towards the United States. In the war between those new Governments and Spain, we declared our neutrality, at the time of their recognition, and to this we have adhered, and, shall continue to adhere, provided no change shall occur, which in the judgement of the competent authorities of this Government, shall make a corresponding change, on the part of the United States, indispensable to their security.

The late events in Spain and Portugal, shew that Europe is still unsettled. Of this important fact, no stronger proof can be adduced, than that the allied powers should have thought it proper, on any principle satisfactory to themselves, to have interposed by force, in the internal concerns of Spain. To what extent, such interposition may be carried, on the same principle, is a question, in which all Independent powers, whose Governments differ from theirs, are interested; even those most remote, and surely none more so than the United States. Our

44

policy in regard to Europe, which was adopted at an early stage of the wars which have so long agitated that quarter of the Globe, nevertheless remains the same, which is, not to interfere in the internal concerns of any of its powers; to consider the Government de facto, as the legitimate for us; to cultivate friendly relations with it, and to preserve those relations, by a frank, firm and manly policy, meeting in all instances, the just claims of every power; submitting to injuries from none. But, in regard to those continents, circumstances are eminently and conspicuously different. It is impossible that the allied powers should extend their political system to any portion of either continent without endangering our peace and happiness; nor can any one believe that our Southern brethern, if left to themselves, would adopt it of their own accord. It is equally impossible, therefore, that we should behold such interposition, in any form, with indifference. If we look to the comparative strength and resources of Spain and those new Governments, and their distance from each other, it must be obvious that she can never subdue them. It is still the true policy of the United States to leave the parties to themselves, in the hope that other powers will pursue the same course . . .

EMANCIPATION PROCLAMATION

This proclamation, issued on January 1, 1863, freed the slaves in the territory in rebellion against the United States. It did not abolish slavery; that required a constitutional amendment. The original proclamation, bearing Lincoln's signature and the seal of the United States, is in the National Archives at Washington.

17

By the President of the United States of America: A Proclamation.

Whereas, on the twenty-second day of September, in the year of our Lord one thousand eight hundred and sixty-two, a proclamation was issued by the President of the United States, containing, among other things, the following, to wit:

"That on the first day of January, in the year of our Lord one thousand eight hundred and sixty-three, all persons held as slaves within any State or designated part of a State, the people whereof shall then be in rebellion against the United States, shall be then, thenceforward, and forever free; and the Executive Government of the United States, including the military and naval authority thereof, will recognize and maintain the freedom of such persons, and will do no act or acts to repress such persons, or any of them, in any efforts they may make for their actual freedom.

"That the Executive will; on the first day of January aforesaid, by proclamation, designate the States and parts of States, if any, in which the people thereof respectively shall then be in rebellion against the United States; and the fact that any State, or the people thereof, shall on that day be in good faith represented in the Congress of the United States by members chosen thereto at elections wherein a majority of the qualified voters of such State shall have participated, shall in the absence of strong countervailing testimony be deemed conclusive evidence that such State and the people thereof are not then in rebellion against the United States."

Now, therefore, I, Abraham Lincoln, President of the United States, by virtue of the power in me vested as commander-in-chief of the army and navy of the United States, in time of actual armed rebellion against the authority and government of the United States, and as a fit and necessary war measure for suppressing said rebellion, do, on this first day of January, in the year of our Lord one thousand eight hundred and sixty-three, and in accordance with my purpose so to do, publicly proclaimed for the full period of 100 days from the day first above mentioned, order and designate as the States and parts of States wherein the people thereof, respectively, are this day in rebellion against the United States, the following, to wit:

Arkansas, Texas, Louisiana (except the parishes of St. Bernard, Plaquemines, Jefferson, St. John, St. Charles, St. James, Ascension, Assumption, Terre Bonne, Lafourche. St. Mary, St. Martin, and Orleans, including the city of New Orleans), Mississippi, Alabama, Florida, Georgia, South Carolina, North Carolina, and Virginia (except the forty-eight counties designated as West Virginia, and also the counties of Berkeley, Accomac, Northampton, Elizabeth City, York, Princess Ann, and Norfolk, including the cities of Norfolk and Portsmouth), and which excepted parts are for the present left precisely as if this proclamation were not issued.

And by virtue of the power and for the purpose aforesaid, I do order and declare that all persons held as slaves within said designated States and parts of States are, and henceforward shall be, free; and that the Executive Government of the United States, including the military and naval authorities thereof, will recognize and maintain the freedom of said persons.

And I hereby enjoin upon the people so declared to be free to abstain from all violence, unless in necessary self-defense; and I recommend to them that, in all cases when allowed, they labor faithfully for reasonable wages.

And I further declare and make known that such persons of suitable condition will be received into the armed service of the United States to garrison forts, positions, stations, and other places, and to man vessels of all sorts in said service. And upon this act, sincerely believed to be an act of justice, warrented by the Constitution upon military necessity, I invoke the considerate judgment of mankind and the gracious favor of Almighty God.

In witness whereof, I have hereunto set my hand, and caused the seal of the United States to be affixed.

Done at the City of Washington, this first day of January, in the year of our Lord one thousand eight hundred and sixty three, and of the Independence of the United States of America the eighty-seventh.

Abraham Lincoln

By the President:
William H. Seward,
Secretary of State.

THE GETTYSBURG ADDRESS

The reading copy of the Gettysburg Address, in Lincoln's own handwriting, which he held as he delivered the address on November 19, 1863, is reproduced here. The original belongs to the Library of Congress at Washington.

18

Four score and seven years ago our fathers brought forth, upon this continent, a new nation, conceived in Liberty, and dedicated to the proposition that all men are created equal.

Now we are engaged in a great civil war, testing whether that nation, or any nation, so conceived, and so dedicated, can long endure. We are met here on a great battle-field of that war. We have come to dedicate a portion of it as a final resting place for those who here gave their lives that that nation might live. It is altogether fitting and proper that we should do this.

But in a larger sense we can not dedicate — we can not consecrate — we can not hallow this ground. The brave men, living and dead, who struggled here, have consecrated it far above our poor power to add or detract. The world will little note, nor long remember, what we say here, but can never forget what they did here. It is for us, the living, rather to be dedicated here to the unfinished work which they have, thus far, so nobly carried on. It is rather for us to be here dedicated to the great task remaining before us — that from these honored dead we take increased devotion to that cause for which they here gave the last full measure of devotion — that we here highly resolve that these dead shall not have died in vain; that this nation shall have a new birth of freedom; and that this government of the people, by the people, for the people, shall not perish from the earth.

LINCOLN'S SECOND INAUGURAL ADDRESS

Lincoln's brief, intensely moving message, delivered March 4, 1865, a few weeks prior to his assassination, indicts "American Slavery" as the cause of the civil conflict, and an offense against God who "gives to both North and South this terrible war as the woe due to those by whom the offense came." His charity, compassion and greatness as a man and President shine forth in this address, particularly in the immortal closing paragraph. The original manuscript is in the Library of Congress.

19

Fellow Countrymen:

At this second appearing, to take the oath of the presidential office, there is less occasion for an extended address than there was at the first. Then a statement, somewhat in detail, of a course to be pursued, seemed fitting and proper. Now, at the expiration of four years, during which public declarations have been constantly called forth on every point and phase of the great contest which still absorbs the attention, and engrosses the energies of the nation, little that is new could be presented. The progress of our arms, upon which all else chiefly depends, is as well known to the public as to myself; and it is, I trust, reasonably satisfactory and encouraging to all. With high hope for the future, no prediction in regard to it is ventured.

On the occasion corresponding to this four years ago, all thoughts were anxiously directed to an impending civil war. All dreaded it — all sought to avert it. While the inaugural address was being delivered from this place, devoted altogether to saving the Union without war, insurgent agents were in the city seeking to destroy it without war — seeking to dissolve the Union, and divide effects, by negotiation. Both parties deprecated war; but one of them would make war rather then let the nation survive; and the other would accept war rather than let it perish. And the war came.

One eighth of the whole population were colored slaves, not distributed generally over the Union, but localized in the Southern part of it. These slaves constituted a peculiar and powerful interest. All knew that this interest was, somehow, the cause of the war. To strengthen, perpetuate, and extend this interest was the object for which the insurgents would rend the Union, even by war; while the government claimed no right to do more than to restrict the territorial enlargement of it. Neither party expected for the war, the Magnitude, or the duration, which it has already attained. Neither anticipated that the cause of the conflict might cease with, or even before, the conflict itself should cease. Each looked for an easier triumph, and a result less fundamental and astounding. Both read the same Bible, and pray to the same God; and each invokes His aid against the other. It may seem strange that any men should dare to ask a just God's assistance in wringing their bread from the sweat of other men's faces; but let us judge not that we be not judged. The prayers of both could not be answered; that of neither has been answered fully. The Almighty has His own purposes. "Woe unto the world because of offences! for it must needs be that offences come; but woe to that man by whom the offence cometh!" If we shall suppose that American-Slavery is one of those offences which, in the providence of God, must needs come, but which, having continued through His appointed time, He now wills to remove, and that He gives to both North and South, this terrible war, as the woe due to those by whom the offence came, shall we discern therein any departure from those divine attributes which the believers in a living God always ascribe to Him? Fondly do we hope — fervently do we pray — that this mighty scourge of war may speedily pass away. Yet, if God wills that it continue, until all the wealth piled by the bond-man's two hundred and fifty years of unrequited toil shall be sunk, and until every drop of blood drawn with the lash, shall be paid by another drawn with the sword, as was said three thousand years ago, so still it must be said "the judgments of the Lord, are true and righteous altogether"

With malice toward none; with charity for all; with firmness in the right, as God gives us to see the right, let us strive on to finish the work we are in; to bind up the nation's wounds; to care for him who shall have borne the battle, and for his widow, and his orphans to do all which may achieve and cherish a just and lasting peace, among ourselves, and with all nations.

ROBERT E. LEE'S LETTER ACCEPTING THE PRESIDENCY OF WASHINGTON COLLEGE

In a letter of August 24, 1865, to a committee of the Board of Trustees of Washington College, General Lee notified them of his acceptance of the presidency of the college because he thought it "the duty of every citizen in the present condition of the country, to do all in his power to aid in the restoration of peace and harmony." The original letter belongs to Washington and Lee University at Lexington, Va.

20

Powhatan Co: 24 Aug '65

Gentlemen

I have delayed for some days, replying to your letter of the 5 Inst: informing me of my election by the Board of Trustees, to the Presidency of Washington College, from a desire to give the subject due Consideration. Fully impressed with the responsibilities of the office, I have feared that I should be unable to discharge its duties, to the satisfaction of the Trustees, or to the benefit of the Country. The proper education of youth requires not only great ability, but I fear more strength than I now possess, for I do not feel able to undergo the labour of Conducting Classes in regular Courses of instruction. I Could not therefore undertake more than the general administration & supervision of the Institution. There is another subject which has Caused me serious reflection, & is I think worthy of the Consideration of the Board. Being excluded from the terms of amnesty in the proclamation of the President of the U. S. of the 29 May last, & an object of censure to a portion of the Country, I have thought it probable that any occupation of the position of President, might draw upon the College a feeling of hostility; & I should therefore Cause injury to an Institution, which it would be my highest desire to advance. I think it the duty of every Citizen in the present Condition of the Country, to do all in his power to aid in the restoration of peace & harmony, & in no way to oppose the policy of the State or Genl Governments, directed to that object. It is particularly incumbent on those charged with the instruction of the young, to set them an example of submission to authority, & I could not Consent to be the Cause of animadversion upon the College.

Should you however take a different view, & think that my services in the position tendered me by the Board will be advantageous to the College & Country, I will yield to your judgment & accept it. Otherwise I must most respectfully decline the office.

Begging you to express to the trustees of the College my heartfelt gratitude for the honors Conferred upon me, & requesting you to accept my

Cordial thanks for the kind manner in which you have Communicated its decision,

I am Gent^n with great respect
your most obl sert
RE Lee

Messrs John W. Brockenbrough Rector
S. McD Reid, Alfred Leyburn
Horatio Thompson,
D.D. Bolivar Christian
T.J. Kirkpatrick

⎫
⎬ Committee
⎭

50

THE THIRTEENTH AMENDMENT

The Thirteenth Amendment to the Constitution abolished slavery throughout the United States. It was adopted on December 18, 1865, when the last of the necessary number of States ratified it. The original amendment in the usual form of a Joint Resolution of Congress, approved February 1, 1865, is in the National Archives at Washington.

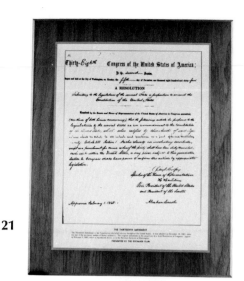

Thirty-Eighth Congress of the United States of America; At the — Second _____ Session, Begun and held at the City of Washington, on Monday, the fifth __ day of December, one thousand eight hundred and sixty-four.

A RESOLUTION

Submitting to the legislatures of the several States a proposition to amend the Constitution of the United States.

Resolved by the Senate and House of Representatives of the United States of America in Congress assembled, (two-thirds of both houses concurring), that the following article be proposed to the legislatures of the several States as an amendment to the Constitution. of the United States, which, when ratified by three-fourths of said Legislatures shall be valid, to all intents and purposes, as a part of the said Constitution, namely: Article XIII. Section 1. Neither slavery nor involuntary servitude, except as a punishment for crime whereof the party shall have been duly convicted, shall exist within the United States, or any place subject to their jurisdiction. Section. 2. Congress shall have power to enforce this article by appropriate legislation.

Schuyler Colfax
Speaker of the House of Representatives.
H. Hamlin
Vice President of the United States.
and President of the Senate.
Abraham Lincoln
Approved, February 1. 1865.

21

THEODORE ROOSEVELT LETTER ON CUBA

On January 22, 1907, President Theodore Roosevelt wrote to Secretary of War William Howard Taft rejecting the idea of a protectorate over Cuba and expressing his determination that the United States should withdraw from the Island as promised. The original letter is in the National Archives at Washington.

22

THE WHITE HOUSE
WASHINGTON
Personal.

January 22, 1907.

My dear Mr. Secretary:

In reference to Magoon's two letters of the 13th and 16th, which are returned herewith, I need hardly add to what I said this morning. There can be no talk of a protectorate by us. Our business is to establish peace and order on a satisfactory basis, start the new government, and then leave the Island; the Cuban Government taking the reins into its own hands; tho of course it might be advisable for some little time that some of our troops should stay in the Islands to steady things. I will not even consider the plan of a protectorate, or any plan which would imply our breaking our explicit promise because of which we were able to prevent a war of devastation last fall. The good faith of the United States is a mighty valuable asset and must not be impaired.

Sincerely yours,
Theodore Roosevelt

Hon. Wm. H. Taft,
    Secretary of War.
Enclosures.

WILSON'S FIRST INAUGURAL ADDRESS

Enunciating his program for social justice, conservation of natural resources and economic reforms, Wilson's Inaugural, delivered March 4, 1913, has been characterized as a great testament of democratic faith. Wilson's letter to George Dobbin Brown, also reproduced, authenticates the document as Wilson's personally typewritten transcript of his original shorthand notes. The original manuscript is in the Princeton University Library.

23

INAUGURAL

There has been a change of government. It began two years ago, when the House of Representatives became Democratic by a decisive majority. It has now been completed. The Senate about to assemble will also be Democratic. The offices of President and Vice President have been put into the hands of Democrats. What does the change mean? That is the question that is uppermost in our minds to-day. That is the question I am going to try to answer, in order, if I may, to interpret the occasion.

It means much more than the mere success of a party. The success of a party means little except when the nation is using that party for a large and definite purpose. No one can mistake the purpose for which the nation now seeks to use the Democratic party. It seeks to use it to interpret a change in its own plans and point of view. Some old things with which we had grown familiar, and which had begun to creep into the very habit of our thought and of our lives, have altered their aspect as we have latterly looked critically upon them, with fresh, awakened eyes; have dropped their disguises and shown themselves alien and sinister. Some new things, as we look frankly upon them, willing to comprehend their real character, have come to assume the aspect of things long believed in and familiar, stuff of our own convictions. We have been refreshed by a new insight into our own life.

We see that in many things that life is very great. It is incomparably great in its material aspects, in its body of wealth, in the diversity and sweep of its energy, in the industries which have been conceived and built up by the genius of individual men and the limitless enterprise of groups of men. It is great, also, very great, in its moral force. Nowhere else in the world have noble men and women exhibited in more striking forms the beauty and the energy of sympathy and helpfulness and counsel in their efforts to rectify wrong, alleviate suffering, and set the weak in the way of strength and hope. We have built up, moerover, a great system of government, which has stood through a long age as in many respects a model for those who seek to set liberty upon foundations that will endure against fortuitous change, against storm and accident. Our life contains every great thing, and contains it in rich abundance.

But evil has come with the good, and much fine gold has been corroded. With riches has come inexcusable waste. We have squandered a great part of what we might have used, and have not stopped to conserve the exceeding bounty of nature without which our genius for enterprise would have been worthless and impotent, scorning to be careful, shamefully prodigal as well as admirably efficient. We have been proud of our industrial achievements, but we have not hitherto stopped thoughtfully enough to count the human cost, the cost of lives snuffed out, of energies overtaxed and broken, the fearful physical and spiritual cost to the men and women and children upon whom the dead weight and burden of it all has fallen pitilessly the years through. The groans and agony of it all had not yet reached our ears, the solemn, moving undertone of our life, coming up out of the mines and factories and out of every home where the struggle had its intimate and familiar seat. With the great government went many deep secret things which we too long delayed to look into and scrutinize with candid, fearless eyes. The great government we loved has too often been made use of for private and selfish purposes, and those who used it had forgotten the people.

At last a vision has been vouchsafed us of our life as a whole. We see the bad with the good, the debased and decadent with the sound and vital. With this vision . . . we approach new affairs. Our duty is to cleanse, to reconsider, to restore, to correct the evil without impairing the good, to purify and humanize every process of our common life without weakening or sentimentalizing it. There has been something crude and heartless and unfeeling in our haste to succeed and be great. Our thought has been "Let every man look out for himself; let every generation look out for itself", while we reared giant machinery which made it impossible that any but those who stood at the levers of control should have a chance to look out for themselves. We had not forgotten our morals. We remembered well enough that we had set up a policy which was meant to serve the humblest as well as the most powerful, with an eye single to the standards of justice and fair play, and remembered it with pride. But we were heedless and in a hurry to be great.

We have come now to the sober second thought. The scales of heedlessness have fallen from our eyes. We have made up our minds to square every process of our national life again with the standards we so proudly set up at the beginning and have always carried at our hearts. Our work is a work of restoration.

We have itemized with some degree of particularity the things that ought to be altered and here are some of the chief items: A tariff which cuts us off from our proper part in the commerce of the world, violates the just principles of taxation, and makes the government a facile instrument in the hands of private interests; a banking and currency system based upon the necessity of the government to sell its bonds fifty years ago and perfectly adapted to concentrating cash and restricting credits; an industrial system which, take it on all its sides, financial as well as administrative, holds capital in leading strings, restricts the liberties and limits the opportunities of labour, and exploits without renewing or conserving the natural resources of the country; a body of agricultural activities never yet given the efficiency of great business undertakings or served as it should be through the instrumentality of science taken directly to the farm, or afforded the facilities of credit best suited to its practical needs; water courses undeveloped, waste places unreclaimed, forests untended, fast disappearing without plan or prospect of renewal, unregarded waste heaps at every mine. We have studied as perhaps no other nation has the most effective means of production, but we have not studied cost or economy as we should either as organizers of industry, as statesmen, or as individuals.

Nor have we studied and perfected the means by which government may be put at the service of humanity, in safeguarding the health of the nation, the health of its men and its women and its children, as well as their rights in the struggle for existence. This is no sentimental duty. The firm basis of government is justice, not pity. These are matters of justice. There can be no equality of opportunity, the first essential of justice in the body politic, if men and women and children be not shielded in their lives, their very vitality, from the consequences of great industrial and social processes which they cannot alter, control, or singly cope with. Society must see to it that it does not itself crush or weaken or damage its own constituent parts. The first duty of law is to keep sound the society it serves. Sanitary laws, pure food laws, and laws determining conditions of labour which individuals are powerless to determine for themselves are intimate parts of the very business of justice and legal efficiency.

These are some of the things we ought to do, and not leave the others undone, the old-fashioned, never to be neglected, fundamental safeguarding of property and of individual right. This is the high enterprise of the new day: to lift everything that concerns our life as a nation to the light that shines from the hearthfire of every man's conscience and vision of the right. It is inconceivable that we should do this as partisans; it is inconceivable we should do it in ignorance of the facts as they are or in blind haste. We shall restore, not destroy. We shall deal with our economic system as it is and as it may be modified, not as it might be if we had a clean sheet of paper to write upon; and step by step we shall make it what it should be, in the spirit of those who question their own wisdom and seek counsel and knowledge, not shallow self-satisfaction or the excitement of excursions whither they cannot tell. Justice, and only justice, shall always be our motto.

And yet it will be no cool process of mere science. The nation has been deeply stirred by a solemn passion, stirred by the knowledge of wrong, of ideals lost, of government too often debauched and made an instrument of evil. The feelings with which we face this new age of right and opportunity sweep across our heartstrings like some air out of God's own presence, where justice and mercy are reconciled and the judge and the brother are one. We know our task to be no mere task of politics but a task which shall search us through and through, whether we be able to understand our time and the need of our people, whether we be indeed their spokesmen and interpreters, whether we have the pure heart to comprehend and the rectified will to choose our high course of action.

This is not a day of triumph; it is a day of dedication. Here muster, not the forces of party, but the forces of humanity. Men's hearts wait upon us, men's lives hang in the balance; men's hopes call upon us to say what we will do. Who shall live up to the great trust? Who dares fail to try? I summon all honest men, all patriotic, all forward-looking men, to my side. God helping me, I will not fail them, if they will but counsel and sustain me!

THE WHITE HOUSE
WASHINGTON

December 10, 1913

My dear Mr. Brown:

I have hunted as much as I had time to hunt among my papers for the real original of my Inaugural address, which was, as you conjecture, written in the Library in shorthand, but I have so far not been able to turn it up. Here is the next to the original, namely, my transcript on my own typewriter from the original shorthand notes. You are quite welcome to put it among the archives if you think it worth it.

Cordially and faithfully yours,
Woodrow Wilson

enc:
Mr. George Dobbin Brown,
Princeton University.

THE NINETEENTH AMENDMENT

The Nineteenth Amendment to the Constitution, giving women the vote, was adopted on August 26, 1920. The original, in the form of a Congressional resolution, is in the National Archives at Washington.

24

5

H. J. Res. 1

Sixty-sixth Congress of the
United States of America;
At the First Session,

Begun and held at the City of Washington, on Monday, the nineteenth day of May, one thousand nine hundred and nineteen.

JOINT RESOLUTION

Proposing an amendment to the Constitution extending the right of suffrage to women.

Resolved by the Senate and House of Representatives of the United States of America in Congress assembled (two-thirds of each House concurring therein), That the following article is proposed as an amendment to the Constitution, which shall be valid to all intents and purposes as part of the Constitution when ratified by the legislatures of three-fourths of the several States.

"Article ——————.

"The right of citizens of the United States to vote shall not be denied or abridged by the United States or by any State on account of sex.

"Congress shall have power to enforce this article by appropriate legislation."

F. H. Gillett —
Speaker of the House of Representatives.
Thos. R. Marshall.
Vice President of the United States and President of the Senate.

SELECTION OF GENERAL EISENHOWER AS SUPREME COMMANDER OF "OVERLORD"

The pencilled note from President Roosevelt to Marshall Stalin stating that the immediate appointment of General Eisenhower to command the Allied invasion of Western Europe — "Overlord" — has been decided upon is reproduced here. It was written by General George C. Marshall and signed by President Roosevelt, and it bears a note of explanation and gift from General Marshall to General Eisenhower.

25

From the President to Marshall Stalin

The immediate appointment of General Eisenhower to command of Overlord operation has been decided upon.

Roosevelt.

Cairo, Dec. 7: 43

Dear Eisenhower, I thought you might like to have this as a memento. It was written very hurriedly by me as the final meeting broke up yesterday, the President signing it immediately.

G.C.M.

McAULIFFE'S CHRISTMAS MESSAGE — 1944

The encouraging Christmas message that Brigadier General Anthony C. McAuliffe sent·to the 101st Airborne Division, surrounded by German units at Bastogne, Belgium, contains his famous reply "Nuts!" to the German demand for surrender. The original belongs to Major General McAuliffe.

26

Headquarters 101st Airborne Division
Office of the Division Commander

24 December 1944

What's Merry about all this, you ask? We're fighting — it's cold — we aren't home. All true but what has the proud Eagle Division accomplished with its worthy comrades of the 10th Armored Division, the 705th Tank Destroyer Battalion and all the rest? Just this: We have stopped cold everything that has been thrown at us from the North, East, South and West. We have identifications from four German Panzer Divisions, two German Infantry Divisions and one German Parachute Division. These units, spearheading the last desperate German lunge, were headed straight west for key points when the Eagle Division was hurriedly ordered to stem the advance. How effectively this was done will be written in history; not alone in our Division's glorious history but in World history. The Germans actually did surround us. their radios blared our doom. Their Commander demanded our surrender in the following impudent arrogance.

December 22nd 1944

"To the U. S. A. Commander of the encircled town of Bastogne.

The fortune of war is changing. This time the U. S. A. forces in and near Bastogne have been encircled by strong German armored units. More German armored units have crossed the river Ourthe near Ortheuville, have taken Marche and reached St. Hubert by passing through Hombres-Sibret-Tillet. Libramont is in German hands.

There is only one possibility to save the encircled U. S. A. Troops from total annihilation: that is the honorable surrender of the encircled town. In order to think it over a term of two hours will be granted beginning with the presentation of this note.

If this proposal should be rejected one German Artillery Corps and six heavy A. A. Battalions are ready to annihilate the U.S.A. Troops in and near Bastogne. The order for firing will be given immediately after this two hour's term.

All the serious civilian losses caused by this Artillery fire would not correspond with the well known American humanity.

The German Commander"

The German Commander received the following reply:

22 December 1944

"To the German Commander:
N U T S !
The American Commander"

Allied Troops are counterattacking in force. We continue to hold Bastogne. By holding Bastogne we assure the success of the Allied Armies. We know that our Division Commander, General Taylor, will say: "Well Done!"

We are giving our country and our loved ones at home a worthy Christmas present and being privileged to take part in this gallant feat of arms are truly making for ourselves a Merry Christmas.

A. C. McAuliffe
McAULIFFE,
Commanding.

THE GERMAN INSTRUMENT OF SURRENDER — WORLD WAR II

The Nazis, who launched World War II in 1939, were forced to surrender in the spring of 1945. It was nearly 3 a.m., 0241 hours, on May 7 at Rheims when the unconditional surrender of "all forces on land, sea, and air" under German control was signed. It provided that military operations were to cease on May 8. The original document is in the National Archives at Washington.

27

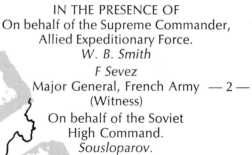

C056077

Only this text in English is authoritative
ACT OF MILITARY SURRENDER

1. We the undersigned, acting by authority of the German High Command, hereby surrender unconditionally to the Supreme Commander, Allied Expeditionary Force and simultaneously to the Soviet High Command all forces on land, sea, and in the air who are at this date under German control.

2. The German High Command will at once issue orders to all German military, naval and air authorities and to all forces under German control to cease active operations at 2301 hours Central European time on 8 May and to remain in the positions occupied at that time. No ship, vessel, or aircraft is to be scuttled, or any damage done to their hull, machinery or equipment.

3. The German High Command will at once issue to the appropriate commanders, and ensure the carrying out of any further orders issued by the Supreme Commander, Allied Expeditionary Force and by the Soviet High Command.

4. This act of military surrender is without prejudice to, and will be superseded by any general instrument of surrender imposed by, or on behalf of the United Nations and applicable to GERMANY and the German armed forces as a whole.

— 1 —

C056078

5. In the event of the German High Command or any of the forces under their control failing to act in accordance with this Act of Surrender, the Supreme Commander, Allied Expeditionary Force and the Soviet High Command will take such punitive or other action as they deem appropriate.

Signed at Rheims at 0241 on the 7th day of May, 1945.   France

On behalf of the German High Command.
Jodl

IN THE PRESENCE OF
On behalf of the Supreme Commander, Allied Expeditionary Force.
W. B. Smith

F Sevez
Major General, French Army — 2 —
(Witness)
On behalf of the Soviet High Command.
Sousloparov.

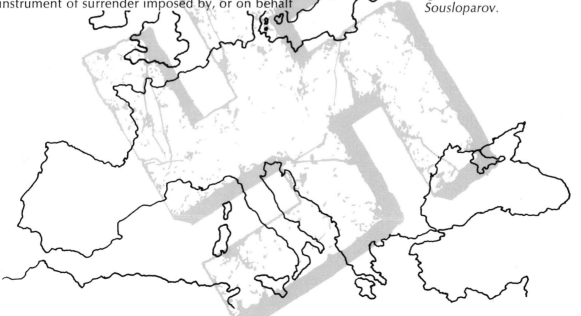

INSTRUMENT OF SURRENDER IN THE PACIFIC — WORLD WAR II

On September 2, 1945, aboard the U. S. S. Missouri in Tokyo Bay, the Japanese surrendered unconditionally, bringing hostilities in World War II to an end. The original instrument of surrender is in the National Archives. at Washington.

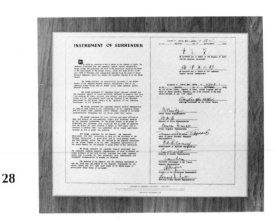

28

INSTRUMENT OF SURRENDER

WE, acting by command of and in behalf of the Emperor of Japan, the Japanese Government and the Japanese Imperial General Headquarters, hereby accept the provisions set forth in the declaration issued by the heads of the Governments of the United States, China and Great Britain on 26 July 1945, at Potsdam, and subsequently adhered to by the Union of Soviet Socialist Republics, which four powers are hereafter referred to as the Allied Powers.

We hereby proclaim the unconditional surrender to the Allied Powers of the Japanese Imperial General Headquarters and of all Japanese armed forces and all armed forces under Japanese control wherever situated.

We hereby command all Japanese forces wherever situated and the Japanese people to cease hostilities forthwith, to preserve and save from damage all ships, aircraft, and military and civil property and to comply with all requirements which may be imposed by the Supreme Commander for the Allied Powers or by agencies of the Japanese Government at his direction.

We hereby command the Japanese Imperial General Headquarters to issue at once orders to the Commanders of all Japanese forces and all forces under Japanese control wherever situated to surrender unconditionally themselves and all forces under their control.

We hereby command all civil, military and naval officials to obey and enforce all proclamations, orders and directives deemed by the Supreme Commander for the Allied Powers to be proper to effectuate this surrender and issued by him or under his authority and we direct all such officials to remain at their posts and to continue to perform their noncombatant duties unless specifically relieved by him or under his authority.

We hereby undertake for the Emperor, the Japanese Government and their successors to carry out the provisions of the Potsdam Declaration in good faith, and to issue whatever orders and take whatever action may be required by the Supreme Commander for the Allied Powers or by any other designated representative of the Allied Powers for the purpose of giving effect to that Declaration.

We hereby command the Japanese Imperial Government and the Japanese Imperial General Headquarters at once to liberate all allied prisoners of war and civilian internees now under Japanese control and to provide for their protection, care, maintenance and immediate transportation to places as directed.

The authority of the Emperor and the Japanese Government to rule the state shall be subject to the Supreme Commander for the Allied Powers who will take such steps as he deems proper to effectuate these terms of surrender.

Signed at TOKYO BAY, JAPAN at 0904. I on the SECOND day of SEPTEMBER, 1945.

Mamoru Shigemitsu
By Command and in behalf of the Emperor of Japan and the Japanese Government.

Yoshijiro Umezu
By Command and in behalf of the Japanese Imperial General Headquarters.

Accepted at TOKYO BAY, JAPAN, at 0908 I on the SECOND day of SEPTEMBER, 1945, for the United States, Republic of China, United Kingdom and the Union of Soviet Socialist Republics, and in the interests of the other United Nations at war with Japan.

Douglas MacArthur
Supreme Commander for the Allied Powers.

C. W. Nimitz
United States Representative

Hsu Yang-Chiang
Republic of China Representative

Bruce. Fraser.
United Kingdom Representative

Kazma Direvyanko
Union of Soviet Socialist Republics Representative

T A Blamey
Commonwealth of Australia Representative

L. Moore Cosgrave
Dominion of Canada Representative

'Le Clerc
Provisional Government of the French Republic Representative

C. E. L. Helfrich
Kingdom of the Netherlands Representative

Leonard M Isitt
Dominion of New Zealand Representative